LORNA
The Peak District Vet

LORNA FRANCIS

First published in Great Britain in 2022 by
Bannister Publications Ltd
118 Saltergate, Chesterfield, Derbyshire S40 1NG

Copyright © Lorna Francis
Illustrations by Lorna Francis

ISBN: 978-1-909813-78-6

A catalogue record for this book is available from the British Library

Typeset in EB Garamond
Printed and bound in Great Britain

This book was self-published by Bannister Publications.
For more information on self-publishing visit:
www.bannisterpublications.com

To
Adèle
for inspiration.

CONTENTS

FOREWORD
BY THE DUCHESS OF DEVONSHIRE

Derbyshire is a very special county and it's often incomers who most vividly realise this.........and then tell everyone what Derbyshire folk know already.

A vet, looking after farm animals as well as pets, is particularly well placed to understand the inwardness of the communities in which they work. The travelling to remote and difficult locations to find farms and villages, at all times of the day and night and at every time of year, has taught the author just how special Derbyshire is, how welcoming, funny and generous most of the community can be, how open and straight they are too, sometimes almost too open with opinions as to the vet's professional ability!

This book, written by Lorna Francis regards it as a privilege to work as a vet: it is full of optimism and good humour but it also explains how hard is the hill farmer's life, how easily their stock or crops can fail and how drastic this always is for the farmer's business. There is little room for sentimentality in farming but that does not mean that the farmers don't love their animals. They look after them with all the care in the world and spend hours sitting with a poorly beast waiting and hoping for an improvement in its health.

Lorna Francis has shared many stories and provided charming sketches from her life as a rural vet and in doing so has painted a wonderful picture of life in the Derbyshire countryside, a truthful picture full of charm and yet never avoiding the hard physical struggle that is the constant feature of the lives of those who create the countryside that the rest of us are able to enjoy.

Amanda Devonshire.

Acknowledgments

Writing and illustrating this book, then experiencing the publishing process and beyond has been fun, exciting and a steep learning curve. Thank you to the people who, directly and indirectly have given their time, advice and support and to all those who have contributed to the subject matter for these pages.

Lorna

INTRODUCTION

Writing this short book has given me an opportunity to share the delights, humour and hardship of living and working as a rural vet, to introduce you to some of the colourful characters who have enriched my veterinary life and for you to vicariously enjoy the pleasures and pride, friendships and laughter I have found living and working in this rural community.

These anecdotes are events as I remember them: true or altered by years of memory or somewhere in between the two. The names of the characters have been altered, they are different in these pages from those of the people still living and working here today.

I hope you enjoy reading my book as much as I enjoyed writing it.

CHAPTER ONE

A NEW HOME

I was unfamiliar with Derbyshire until I came to work and live here. It was a county about which I had little knowledge, but I knew I wanted to work as a veterinary surgeon in a rural practice treating livestock as well as pets, and the job advert I answered fitted the bill. At the interview, I was shown around the area by the senior partner and fell in love with the stunning countryside. I was offered the job, and it didn't take long after I moved up here for me to become very fond of the people who call this county home. I found a very down to earth and friendly folk, eager to help a young vet who lacked a lot of experience. The pretty market town of Bakewell had a wealth of independent food shops including several butchers, bakers, a delicatessen and a once-weekly outdoor market selling fresh fruit and vegetables with so many other varied stalls that it must surely be one of the best outdoor markets around. There was a weekly cattle market too, so on Mondays there was a real buzz in the town as farmers bought and sold stock in the auction and enjoyed 'chewing the fat' with their neighbours and catching up on farming gossip. I've used the past tense in this description to depict the town I saw when I first moved here. Luckily, many of these things still ring true in Bakewell today.

A farm vet's daily routine involves driving to different farms or holdings to check over the stock, to examine and treat animals who are sick or in difficulty, advise on disease prevention and control and many more unusual jobs besides. It is a very efficient way of getting to know one's way around the small country lanes. You soon learn the shortest route to and between different areas of the practice, you are privileged to see the seasons unfold, to catch glimpses of dramatic scenery, stunning views and to experience Derbyshire weather in all its forms through hailstorms and rain in the hills to sheltered sunny corners in the dales. I swiftly learnt which villages had the best local shops and which shops sold the best snacks. There was a renowned pork butcher who sold pies still hot from the oven. They were filled with chunks of pork, and the pastry was crusty and warm and delicious. I knew where to park to avoid the traffic warden while I ran to the shop, bought a pie and ran back to the car. I always intended to eat half the pie while it was still warm and keep the rest for later. Without fail, I had demolished the entire pie before I had arrived at my first call!

Derbyshire farmers are very hospitable, and I was frequently asked into the farmhouse for a cup of tea and a piece of cake after completing the task at hand. One of my favourite memories is of an elderly lady who baked her own currant loaves. Her son still lived at home, farmed the land and looked after the cattle; he would show me which animal I had come to see. Sometimes it would be a cow that was 'off its food' or perhaps a few calves to 'disbud' – remove their tiny horn buds before they grow into horns and give the cows a weapon to use when fighting amongst themselves. Then we would go indoors for a 'cuppa' brewed on the black range, and a thick slice of currant bread generously spread with butter. Most of the farms I visited were family farms, where the family lived on the farm and did the work there. Just a few were farms owned by a more distant business and run day to day by a stockperson. It was not the norm to be invited into the house for a cup of tea at these farms, but I've often shared a mug of tea in the office while talking over a health plan or looking at health records and discussing what action to take.

I found, and still find Derbyshire folk to be very accepting. One of the wonderful things about being a country vet is the bond you build up with your farming clients. The work is often hard and dirty and can take place in antisocial hours. You have to think on your feet and be prepared to give your utmost both physically and mentally. You share the worries and joys of the situation together with the farmer. You are dealing with situations the outcome of which has huge financial and emotional consequences for the farm and the family. Being in this together creates a bond that is lasting. Working with your colleagues at the practice, you enjoy a similar team spirit.

You pull together and work through the hard times and experience the joy and laughter together. I reflect how lucky I am to have experienced these feelings.

It is hard to recall exactly how long I had lived and worked in Derbyshire before it became the place I thought of as home, but not a lot of time passed before I became aware of a profound sense of belonging, of being accepted by my veterinary colleagues, by the wonderfully diverse spectrum of clients and by the communities in which I worked and lived.

The area that was now my home was happily also home to many friendly local pubs, which gave a focal point for acquaintances to be made and friendships to blossom. One of my favourite hostelries, when I was a young vet in the area, was a traditional country pub in a small village. It had low ceilinged half-timbered rooms whose wooden beams hung with gleaming horse brasses. I never found out who had the job of polishing all this brass, but I certainly didn't envy them. In the smallest room was a cosy open fire, piles of wood neatly stacked on the floor beside it. The room, with its wooden tables and old benches, was warm and welcoming. Dogs too were always welcome, which was great for my faithful rescue dog and me, and we spent many happy times in this pub enjoying the company of friends and learning about village life from the locals. My best friend, my rescue dog was medium sized, long haired, gentle, slightly nervous, very loveable and devoted with beautiful soulful brown eyes; she looked trustingly at me whilst she lay by my feet in front of the fire.

Sleeping peacefully by the fire

One minute she was peacefully in the land of nod, the next minute, she jumped onto her feet and a chilling, loud howling issued forth from her mouth. The whole pub went suddenly silent; it sounded as though someone was being beaten or tortured. I jumped up and tried to soothe her and comfort her, at once worried for her and embarrassed by the commotion we were causing.

At first, I couldn't see what had happened then I noticed a log on the floor where she had been asleep. It had fallen from the pile, and as it had rolled towards her, she had uttered this dreadful cry of fear, the log didn't touch her, but she had anticipated that it might roll onto her and hurt her—my poor little girl. Several hugs and lots of stroking from everyone calmed her down and the rest of the pub went back to their conversations, and we all relaxed once more.

Another favourite rendezvous was a pub nestled in the heart of a small village at the start (or finish) of one of my favourite circular walks. Inside the pub, the small bar was cosy and intimate, while outside tables and chairs waited

invitingly in the shade of a wonderful horse chestnut tree.
Pub lunches could be looked forward to while I walked
the hills and valleys surrounding the inn, or sometimes I
would take a picnic and eat it sitting on the village green
watching the world go by. There may be other walkers
who had similar ideas to me sitting munching a sandwich,
three ducks from the farmyard often waddled past
quacking to themselves keeping a beady eye open for
leftover luncheon morsels, or perhaps the smartly dressed
occupants would venture out from a holiday cottage to
sample the local beer right on their doorstep.

Derbyshire 'squeezes' are just what the word suggests
to walkers in this stone wall countryside. Squeeze stiles
allow one to squeeze through the dry-stone walls from one
field to the next when there is no gate. There are a lot of
squeezes on an average walk through the Derbyshire fields.
They consist of two vertical upright stones, perhaps three
feet high, placed a foot or so apart in the wall leaving a gap
between them through which the path leads. Sometimes if
the gap is very narrow, it is necessary to swing through,
taking your weight on your arms, one on each stone
upright. Dogs can often walk straight through unhindered
or jump over the whole thing as the squeeze is usually

lower than the surrounding wall. Some small dogs squash down to 'crawl' through, especially if the stones have tilted and are leaning towards each other at the top. In her older years, when my dog was no longer capable of leaping like a puppy, I would find myself building up my muscles lifting her over a stile that she could no longer negotiate in one springy jump.

Some of the Derbyshire stiles have a different design, a wooden ladder standing like an 'A' bridging the three-foot-high dry-stone wall. Each side has three or four steps, which may be flat, narrow wooden platforms or more precarious natural rounded logs. There is a flat platform placed directly above the wall at the apex of the stile. Attempting to carry a collie size dog over one of these stiles, even when the dog is very placid and doesn't struggle or squirm in your arms, is rather hazardous – for dog and for owner. One afternoon on my half-day off, my faithful dog and I were making our way down the steep sides of a limestone valley, through fields of grazing sheep. We were heading down towards a tea shop that had recently been opened in a restored mill by the river running a long way below us in the valley bottom. It was getting late, the tea shop would soon be closing, so I was hurrying, driven onwards by the thought of homemade cakes or perhaps a scone thickly spread with bramble jam made from the large juicy blackberries that were so plentiful in the woods this year. It was with dismay I realised the only way out of the field was over the tallest ladder stile I had ever seen. There was no gate in sight; I didn't want to retrace my steps back up the hill to try to find an alternative route and risk the cafe being closed when I reached it. I decided I would have to summon all my strength, and my dog and I would have to scale the dizzy heights of the stile together. I picked her up, hugging her tightly to my chest; I could only just see over the top of her back. With a mighty effort, I climbed up the ladder, forming one side of the stile, I had to lean forward toward the stile and wall in order to keep my balance and not fall off backwards. I wished I could hold on to the wooden steps, but I couldn't as both arms were firmly clasped around my trusting dog.

Once on top, I forced myself not to look down lest I got vertigo from being such a height above the dry-stone wall. Slowly but surely, we progressed down the far side, and then we were there standing on terra firma once more. Shakily I lowered the dog to the ground; she turned to give me a quick look as if to say, "What on earth was that all about?" then she set off down the hill with me in hot pursuit towards that well-earned cake and tea.

My faithful dog lived to a ripe old age, but when she passed away, I missed her dreadfully and missed the companionship a dog provides so, after a while, I decided I was ready to think about a successor. I eventually decided to get a smaller dog, a terrier, something completely different, so not only would direct comparisons be less likely, but I would learn at first hand the characteristics of a totally different type and breed. It is an easy job to pick this little terrier up and pop him over a stile or to tuck him under my arm as I climb a ladder stile.

It is easy too to lift a terrier into the back of a car. If you have a large dog that can't or won't do as bidden, it may be necessary to resort to guile. Many 'pickup trucks' are high off the ground, easy enough for a youthful collie dog to bound into the back and travel in style but impossible if the hound in question is large, rather weighty and not given to obeying his owner. The owner of the aforementioned hound frequently had cause to bring Benji to the surgery, and each time she came to leave, Benji led her a dance. She had acquired a sturdy wooden ramp complete with anti-slip crossbars, which was placed against the back of the pickup while the unwilling hound inched his way down from the back of the truck and was led reluctantly into the surgery waiting room, ramp remaining in position at the tail end of the truck. At the end of Benji's visit, it was a very different story. When the pair came to depart, Benji would not walk back up the ramp; he would hardly even deign to look disparagingly at the ramp. The owner would push, pull, place titbits in a line up the ramp, place Benji's front paws on the bottom of the ramp but all to no avail, thirty minutes later, they would still be in the car park, Benji looking unperturbed, the owner becoming a little fractious. At last, the owner would agree to accept a helping hand, and several of the practice team lifted Benji unceremoniously into the truck. Only for it all to be repeated at the next visit.

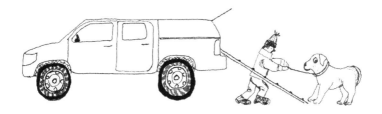

CHAPTER TWO

DO YOU FANCY SOME EGGS AND BACON?

Derbyshire is an area of dramatic heather-clad moors, vertical gritstone edges, rolling pastureland and limestone dales. Each area has its own distinctive landscape and flora. I particularly love the cowslips which carpet the steep-sided dales in spring and the bluebells which carpet the woods with a dazzling brightness and pervade the air with perfume. The area has its own style of small hill farms worked tirelessly by farming folk, many of whom could be classed as local characters. Working together through difficult times, in hard physical situations, often in the dead of night or very early morning when other people (one could say sensible folk) aren't working builds a strong bond. This bond is something valuable in our profession, something I feel privileged to have experienced so many times.

Bluebells

It is with delight that I recall many people on the farms who showed me kindness and helped me. The scenarios I recall are often humorous, some more so in retrospect than at the time!

Many stories involve cups of tea and a few recall visits to the toilet. When you've been out on a long morning's round of calls and had more than one mug of tea since breakfast, visiting the toilet becomes a necessity. One farm was an icon of years gone by; the kettle still warmed over the range, a side of ham hung from the ceiling and loomed over the kitchen table, faded, peeling paper covered the kitchen walls. Outside the cows were still tethered by their necks in rows in the byre and all had individual names: Little Orange, because her Mum had been called Orange and she was a small calf, or Crinkle Ear because that was how her ear was shaped, and then there was Crumple Horn because she had grown a small, crumpled horn where she had been disbudded. The sisters were the farmers here and worked long, hard days. They tried to keep warm in the harsh winters by each wearing several coats, one on top of the other, forming many layers tied round with baler twine, and keeping their head warm would be a fur bonnet that once long ago would have been fashionable. They had a blue merle collie dog for working the cattle; he had a pretty, grey coat and pale blue, almost white eyes. He was good at his work, but he hated vets, and I was frightened of him. He was tied up in a corner of the yard and barked and snarled at me, showing his very white and very pointed teeth. On this particular day, I was examining a cow that had 'gone off her food'; I was worried she may have a displaced stomach, a condition which can be detected by listening with a stethoscope for a characteristic pinging sound. Luckily, when I examined her, I determined she wasn't suffering from a displaced stomach, but she did have an infection in her uterus following calving. I was able to successfully treat her and afterwards was washing my boots and over trousers when, probably brought on by the sound of running water, I knew I would have to ask where the toilet was. On previous visits I had been invited into the kitchen so knew not to expect a state-of-the-art bathroom but was surprised to be directed to a tumbledown shed round the back of the yard. Horror of horrors, I had to walk right past the Hound of the Baskervilles to get there. I could see his chain was only joined to his collar by a thin piece of frayed string. I was terrified. I crept past and reached the shed unscathed. Pushing open the door, I saw there was a metal bucket with a seat attached. That was all. There was no water for flushing or washing, just a bucket in a strongly smelling shed guarded by a vet-eating growling dog. I didn't dare to wonder if there was a flushing toilet in the house that I could try to find; I was too worried a ferocious hound would come bounding through the door which wouldn't close properly and I would be found bitten and mauled, over trousers round ankles unable to flee.

Of course, this never happened. I was very relieved in more ways than one.

O ne day I had to visit a farm nestled in the bottom of a pretty wooded valley. They had a cow having difficulty calving and needed help. I was warned the drive was 'a bit steep', but this turned out to be a complete understatement. I've never before or since had the experience of driving down what felt like a scenic railway – narrow, rutted, so steep I wondered if my brakes would stop me at the bottom or if I'd go careering bonnet first into the stream that ran through the muddy farmyard.

I made it safely to the farm, a picturesque cottage with the stream in front and stone barns to the side. I put on my full-length waterproof smock, lubricated my arms and felt inside the cow. I could feel a tail, nothing else but a tail. This meant the calf's back legs were facing forwards, it was the wrong way round, and its legs were tucked underneath it rather than stuck out backwards. It would not be able to be delivered in this position; I would have to correct the position of the calf inside the cow. I injected the cow to stop her from having contractions, then pushed the calf back into the cow and felt for first one hind leg and then the other and carefully repositioned them, then straightened them out behind the calf. Once in the correct position for a backwards birth, I was able to deliver a lovely live calf. We rubbed it down with straw and let the mother lick it and form a bond. It's a lovely sight when you have a newly born calf and a very attentive mother cow.

I was asked into the farmhouse for a cup of tea which I readily accepted; I think we'd all earned a brew! When I'd arrived in the yard, I'd noticed several healthy-looking chickens clucking around outside the back door, which isn't an unusual thing to see in such a setting. I was more surprised to see a large pile of used teabags outside the back door, presumably awaiting their journey to the bin or compost. I climbed up the three worn stone steps to the kitchen door and entered. It was lovely and warm, an old-fashioned range on which a kettle was boiling glowed on one side of the small room. There was a frying pan on top of the range. It was a well-used frying pan with a generous layer of fat in it, betraying many a cooked breakfast enjoyed over recent days. I looked at the frying pan and blinked, and looked again. Standing in the frying pan, pecking at the fat, was a great big brown hen! The farmer's wife shooed it away, put the pan on the heat and asked me if I'd like some eggs and bacon...

CHAPTER THREE
PLEASE COULD YOU REPEAT THAT?

The newly born twin calves lay side by side in the clean straw of the barn; their mum, a black and white dairy cow, slowly began to lick them dry after their entrance into the world on this cold and frosty night. The farmer had called me out when he realised there were too many legs coming at once, and the cow needed assistance quickly before it was too late. When I felt inside the cow, I could feel two calves both trying to come out together, which would be impossible. After sorting out which legs belonged to which calf, I was able to push one calf back deeper into the uterus; then, when the cow pushed, I could help the other calf to be born. Now there were two bonny black and white calves looking around with their big eyes. I felt back inside the cow to make sure all was as it should be, to check there were no cuts or bleeding. I could feel no problems. But imagine my surprise, when feeling into the very depths of the uterus, a good warm arm's length inside the cow I could feel another leg!

"Good heavens, I think we've got triplets", I blurted out.

"I've only seen one set afore an' that was when me dad was farming, and I was a little un" was the farmer's surprised response.

This was a first for me, life as a vet is always full of new experiences, and this was one of the very best because soon there were three new calves being licked by the proud mum. I was able to go back home to bed feeling very satisfied.

The following week fame awaited when I opened the local newspaper to see a picture of me with three newly born black and white calves and a proud mother cow looking on.

"She's crambly on 'er feet n she's a crozzly pap-end, can you come and tek a look she's our best cow?" The voice sounded old and gnarled and incredibly difficult to decipher even on the third repetition.

The dialect was like a foreign language to me. I had no idea what I was going to see or what might be wrong with the cow when I arrived at a handsome three-storey stone farmhouse in a small sleepy hamlet early one morning. Two elderly brothers still farmed a few head of stock here. The farm had been in their family for generations, and they were the last of the line. They milked a handful of cows and had some sheep. This wouldn't make anything like a living for them, but this was their life, and like so many folks who have lived on and with the land and its animals, they don't want to give up doing what they have always done and loved. Their 'best' cow was a Blue Albion, an old breed not seen so much these days; in fact, this breed is on the rare breed list now, having fewer than 150 breeding females.

Blue Albions were originally called 'Bakewell Blues', originating in Derbyshire; I only remember one other client having some of this breed.

She was tied up in a shippon, which was the main type of cattle housing before loose yards and cubicle sheds. The latter give the cows more freedom to roam around over the winter months, when they are housed inside to protect the fields from poaching (being churned up by hooves when the ground is soft and wet) and protect the cattle from the wind, rain and snow that can lash these hills and dales for several weeks of the year. That has reminded me of another story, but more of that later.

Watching the cow hobble out of the shippon (or stone barn), I could see that 'crambly' was a good description of her walk; she looked as though she was tottering over hot coals. She really didn't want to put each foot down, but when you're a 500Kg cow with four legs and four hooves, you certainly can't hop. So, if you have several sore feet, you are in a pickle when you need to walk, and you put each foot down as gingerly as you can and progress across the farmyard in a, well in a 'crambly' sort of way. Poor girl, she was having rather too good a diet, and it was making her feet very tender and being a bit portly too didn't help her at all.

As to her 'crozzly pap end', it was only when I was shown the scab on the end of her teat, which made it very hard to milk her, did I put two and two together and understand the description. This was a privileged opportunity to experience a scene from life from a bygone time.

The Blue Albion cow recovered. She was no longer crambly or crozzly!

CHAPTER FOUR
CELEBRATIONS

One of the favourite pets I treated was a Bassett Hound called Amy; she had long dangly ears and a mournful face. She was always very friendly, and her owner Daphne said what a lovely companion she was. One day Amy came into the clinic looking very sorry for herself. She had been sick several times and wasn't interested in anything going on around her, which was very out of character for Amy, who usually kept a keen eye on all the comings and goings in her house. I checked her over and felt in her abdomen; it didn't feel as it should do, so we decided to take an x-ray of the area to confirm what we were beginning to suspect. Amy had a blockage in her intestinal tract; we would need to operate and see what was causing the stoppage. Any delay and Amy's condition would rapidly deteriorate, and surgery would become a greater risk than it already was.

Once Amy was anaesthetised and on the operating table, I opened her abdomen and had a look to see what was causing the problem. I carefully felt all along the guts until I located the foreign body firmly lodged in the small intestine. It had a vaguely familiar mushroom shape, just perfect for getting stuck; I cut over it and gently pulled it free; it was covered in partially digested food material that was rather slimy and was a funny shape. I handed it to my nurse for her to clean it up and discover what it was. It turned out to be a Champagne cork; Amy must have very high-quality taste.

Amy made a full recovery. Daphne was very pleased to have her companion back to full fitness but was very embarrassed that Amy had managed to find a Champagne cork on the floor!

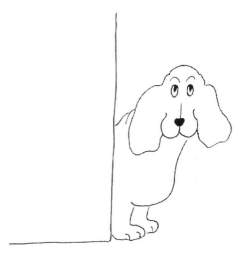

Amy recovered well following the removal of the Champagne cork

There is a moral to this tale which is never to leave the cork lying around after you open a bottle of wine, always remember to put the cork safely into the bin, or you may find yourself down at the vets with a very poorly pet.

It's not only Champagne corks that disappear down dog's throats in the twinkling of an eye. I have had to surgically remove corn cobs which pass out from the stomach and soon become wedged in the smaller diameter intestine leading to disaster unless promptly removed.

On another occasion, I remember a kitten who thought it great sport to sort through her owner's sewing kit and play with the cotton thread, blissfully unaware of the needle that was attached to one end of the thread. The owner wasn't sure if the kitten had actually swallowed anything out of the sewing box but luckily realised that there may have been a needle and thread in the box, and these could no longer be found anywhere in the spilt contents adorning the lounge floor. A visit to the vet and an x-ray confirmed the needle was now inside the kitten. Cotton sewing thread does not show up on x-ray but can be very serious indeed when swallowed as it causes the intestines to concertina into a zig-zag, and the thread passes through the intestine wall many times, holding the guts in this pattern. In the little kitten's case, I was able to operate very early on and remove the offending needle and thread before very serious, or perhaps even fatal damage occurred. A lucky black kitten and an observant owner (who vowed never to leave the sewing box on the lounge floor again). This happened a few years ago, and the kitten grew into a beautiful black cat and lived happily ever after.

It is fair to say more foreign bodies are removed from inside dogs than from cats due to man's best friends' love of food or anything resembling food. Sandy, the dog, was well known at the practice for her habit of pinching food. Her lovely owner tried everything she could to stop Sandy from helping herself to all sorts of delicacies but to no avail. One Christmas Eve was no exception. My afternoon clinic was already full, but I noticed a name had been slipped in as an extra appointment. 'Sandy has eaten something again' was the note on my computer screen. This time she waddled into the surgery with a bulging tummy, and her owner was rather distraught.

"The turkey was defrosting on the table, and Sandy managed to get to it, and she's eaten more than half of it."

No wonder the poor dog was uncomfortable and no wonder the poor owner was unhappy; she had all her family coming round to Christmas lunch in a few hours' time and now had no turkey to feed them. Sandy escaped surgery on this occasion and made an uneventful recovery. The family didn't come off so lightly; they had to have a substitute Christmas lunch and buy another turkey to celebrate New Year instead.

On a different occasion, Sandy distinguished herself by eating a box of chocolate liqueurs complete with wrappers which were deposited around the garden over subsequent days like colourful clues; she ate socks galore when she was a puppy, and the occasional tea towel, most memorable to me was one day when her owner came rushing into the surgery

"Sandy seems fine, but I can't believe what she's done now."

"She jumped up and pulled the washing off the line, she's eaten some more socks and...my bra"

It was difficult to keep a straight face at the mental image conjured up.

I examined Sandy who was showing no ill effects, we decided to monitor her closely as well as closely monitoring everything that passed through her. Sandy never ailed and continued to be fighting fit and then one day I took a phone call from her owner.

"We found the bra; it came through today. I've thrown it into the dog poo bin with everything else."

I breathed a huge sigh of relief.

Dogs steal food that is not meant for them; they experiment with eating their bed (particularly brand new really expensive dog beds); they pinch clothes and think it is a great sport, they find human medication very tempting to eat or can try to poison themselves by eating toxins put out to kill vermin. This can lead to some emergency situations, which are always serious and sometimes have a sad outcome.

One of the happier outcomes concerned a Beagle, a breed that is fixated on food and eating everything it can find. This particular incident happened one evening when I was on call. I received an emergency phone call from a very upset owner whose Beagle had just eaten several slug pellets. The owner had discovered her dog devouring the pellets, and she felt awful because she had put them down to kill the slugs which were treating her vegetables as a Michelin starred restaurant.

I knew I had to see the Beagle as soon as possible and give her a drug to make her vomit. We met at the surgery, the Beagle looking as if butter wouldn't melt in her mouth, but I knew there was a high chance she would start to have seizures if she absorbed the poison. I took her into the consulting room, weighed her and injected the calculated dose of the specific drug. The patient and her owner just made it to the doormat on their way out of the surgery before the Beagle started to heave, and we knew she was going to be sick. Moments later, a mass of bright blue slug pellets was deposited on the doormat. I have rarely been pleased to have to clean up vomit and wash a floor, but that evening I was delighted to know that the Beagle should now be safe.

Rats are a big problem on farms and in barns, where they have access to waste food or bird food that has spilt from feeders. Rat poison is commonly used to control the numbers of these rodents, but all too often is found and eaten by the pet dog. It is always important to let the vet know as much as possible about the poison the pet has eaten (take a label or the container to the surgery with you for details), so treatment can be as effective as possible. I have seen several dogs who have eaten rat poison which can cause ill effects over a long period. It can also be fatal.

One evening when I was on duty, I received a call from a friend who owned a sweet little dog called Hettie. My friend had found Hettie exploring the contents of her handbag on the floor with a strip of Ibuprofen tablets on the carpet beside the bag. Several of the tablets were missing from the blister pack. My friend was sure the strip had been full earlier that day. I was alarmed as I knew that Ibuprofen can be dangerous for dogs, and small dogs only need a small dose to make them very poorly indeed. Hettie was a miniature dog, so adult Ibuprofen tablets were potentially a large overdose to her. I jumped in the car and rushed to the surgery to examine Hettie, who was much quieter than she usually was and give her an injection to make her vomit. There were no Ibuprofen tablets in the vomit. I put Hettie on a drip as it was vital that she didn't become dehydrated and admitted her into the surgery for overnight care. I spent an anxious night worrying about little Hettie and about how my friend must be feeling. Luckily the story had a happy ending. The next morning (which I remember was a Sunday), Hettie was a very bouncy little dog again and could go home feeling fine. My friend was very relieved and so glad to have her little friend home again.

CHAPTER FIVE
PEGGY

It can be cold and windswept looking at stock out in the fields, and the farm I was heading to was in a small village with a commanding view over the hills and dales. The limestone farmhouse looked out onto a tidy yard, and from there you walked to the dairy, the milking parlour and the sheds where the cattle were housed. It was a family farm, Mum and Dad both worked hard, and their two young children both loved helping with the animals and the jobs that needed doing. The farm was very well managed and always really clean and tidy. I had been called to look at a very young calf that was not able to bear weight on one of her front legs; she was in pain and couldn't stand up. This patient would, I knew, be bedded down on clean, deep straw. This wasn't going to be one of those visits when I struggled to keep warm.

The calf was a pretty brown and white Ayrshire heifer, only a few days old. The farmer, Ted, held the calf on her feet while I examined her front leg. The two children looked over the side of the pen. They were concerned as this was a favourite calf.

"What's she done to her leg; can you make her better?" they asked.

"I'm afraid she's broken the bone below her knee, it's called the metacarpal bone, and it's wobbling around so she can't bear any weight on it", I replied, "but I can put a 'pot' on, and it should heal in three or four weeks."

A 'pot' is a cast similar to plaster of Paris; it stops the limb bending and prevents the fractured bone from moving, thus allowing it to heal.

I fetched some rolls of plaster and some pain relief from my car, and we carefully laid the calf on her side in the straw. One person held her head and talked to her. Another person held her hoof out to keep the broken leg straight. I put a soft, comfortable dressing on the leg first, then soaked the plaster bandages in warm water before wrapping them around the leg from top to bottom, with just the lower part of the hoof sticking out. I was careful not to make it too tight; we didn't want it to rub. After a few minutes, the 'pot' was dry, and we lifted the calf, now named Peggy, back onto her feet. She took a few tentative steps then went straight to have a drink of milk from the feeder. I could see she felt better already.

I arranged to come back in three weeks' time to remove the plaster and see if the bone had healed. I crossed my fingers that little Peggy would make a full recovery, and in two years' time, would have a calf of her own and be milked with the rest of the herd to supply milk to a local dairy.

Three weeks later, I drove into the yard again. My emotions were mixed, I wanted to see Peggy and had high hopes for her full recovery, but I was nervous in case the bone hadn't healed as well as I hoped, meaning she would have an uncertain future. The whole family came out to the yard to greet me. Was this a good omen, or the opposite? I was shown into the calf pens. Peggy was on her feet and bawling loudly for food or was it for attention as she had become quite spoilt during the weeks of her recovery. The children had kept her company and stroked her and sat with her; I think they might have even told her a story one day!

I looked down at the cast on her leg. I knew it was no longer going to be pristine white, but I wasn't expecting it to be covered with dirty marks; what were they? I bent down to examine the cast, and as I saw it more clearly, I felt quite emotional. The two children and their friends had each written something on the plaster cast.

"To Peggy, get well soon", "Peggy, lots of love from Lois", "Peg love you lots."

She had to be OK after this. It was with a certain trepidation that I cut down through the cast and prized it away from Peggy's leg like opening up and peeling off a very stiff coat. I felt the leg, bent it extended it, felt the callus where the bone had healed, and yes, it had healed very well. The bone felt strong, and Peggy would be able to start to walk about and run and have a future with the rest of the herd.

"She's healed very well thanks to your care", I happily told the bright, enquiring faces and watched their expressions light up with smiles.

Being a vet can be a very rewarding job.

Peggy the calf with a broken leg

CHAPTER SIX
WHEN THE UNEXPECTED HAPPENS

Spending a considerable amount of time driving along country lanes and up and down rutted farm tracks by day and night, come rain or snow, leads to some interesting and unusual situations. One of my most characterful clients lived in a smallholding comprising a modest stone house forming one side of a courtyard, the other sides of the yard being occupied by stone sheds in varying states of disrepair. One of these sheds housed a few young calves, and it was those I had come to visit. I had been asked to look at some of the calves whose eyes were running and sore. I drove into the yard and got out of the car; several of the calves had their eyes half-closed with copious discharge running down their faces like tears. Their eyes were severely affected by an infectious condition causing ulcers on the cornea, the transparent outer covering of the eyeball. It was important to treat them effectively and quickly in order to save their sight, as well as reduce the pain they were in. I injected antibiotics into each and every eye and arranged to return again to check how they were doing. Some of the calves might need a second injection before they were completely cured.

Preparing to travel from this farm on to my next visit, I got into the car and slowly eased forwards. There was an audible clunk, followed by a none too gentle bump. This was ominous. A heavy jolt and most peculiar noise came from the front wheel. Oh dear, I hoped the car hadn't broken down, for I had a busy day ahead of me and was due to be on call that night too. I certainly hadn't allowed time for a trip to the garage. I got out to check what had happened. I looked at the car, checking nothing had lodged in the wheel arch, but both the wheel and tyre seemed fine; then my eye homed in on an unusual sight behind the wheel half hidden by the car. I could scarcely believe my eyes; it was a kitchen kettle, a kettle like we all use for making tea. A kettle minding its own business on the ground in the middle of the farmyard, and I had driven over it!

The kettle before I ran over it

"Oh, I was wondering where that had got to" Annie, the farmer and kettle owner replied when I recounted what had happened. "The kids must have left it there!"

O n another occasion, I was to learn the hard way that parking very close to a wheelbarrow in the farmyard means that the wheelbarrow handles pointing towards the car are below the driver's line of vision. So, when you get back into your car after several hours of hard work at the farm and drive off quickly to get back to the surgery in time for evening consultations, you drive straight onto the wheelbarrow handles at speed. You then have two substantial dents in your immaculate car.

A lot of my work involved taking blood samples from groups of cattle. Blood samples are taken for diagnostic or monitoring purposes to diagnose the cause of ill health or to try to prevent illness or suboptimal performance before it occurs. One day I was blood testing about fifty heifers (females who have not yet had a calf) who were grazing in a field a few miles distant from the farm. The farmers, Neil and Steve, had been up to the field earlier that morning to prepare for the task and had penned the cattle into a small enclosure so they would be easy to catch when we wanted to sample them. The handling race and examination stall or 'crush' were already in position, so when I drove through the field and parked in the shade of a tree near to the crush, everyone was ready and waiting to start. The blood collecting procedure went smoothly. There was plenty of help to persuade each animal into the crush; I would take a blood sample from the vein running on the underside of the base of the tail, someone else would check the animal's ear tag and write down the number then the heifer would be let out into the field and start to graze on the lush green grass. I would put a label onto the test tube full of blood and cross-reference it with the heifer's ear number before packing the precious samples into a polystyrene box. None of the heifers escaped, so we didn't have to run around the field to get a particular ear tag number back into the pen again, as frequently happens. None of them kicked or behaved badly. Soon I had a box full of blood-filled tubes and a page of completed paperwork. I scrubbed my over trousers and wellingtons, washed my hands and was ready for the off.

Heifers are curious animals by nature and, as expected, had investigated the wing mirrors on my parked car by licking them and covering them with volumes of sticky saliva. But something unexpected had happened as the heifers were standing in the shade watching the last few of their compatriots have their blood samples taken.

There had been a bit of jostling, which I had ignored as this is commonplace among a bunch of playful heifers. But this time, the jostling wasn't all that the heifers had done.

One of the heifers had sat down on my car bonnet.

Now a 400Kg heifer has a substantial backside and leaves a pronounced dent in a shining blue bonnet.

When I came to fill in the insurance claim form, in the section asking me to describe the cause of the damage, I found myself writing, "cow sat on bonnet causing large well-described dent".

To my lasting surprise and relief, the insurance company settled the claim without further questions.

An unusual case was brought into the surgery one day. I ushered the worried owner Eric and his small and very hairy terrier Jack into the surgery. Eric had found a lump on Jack's foot. Jack wouldn't stop licking the lump and had made the area red and sore. He had started to limp a little too and didn't want to go for his usual walk. This was serious because Jack was a mischievous soul who loved racing along the path by the river barking at any other dogs that came into view.

The lump was hard and nestled between two of Jack's toes; it could be something nasty, I would have to investigate. With my nurse's help, we managed to clip all the hair away so we could get a clear view of the lump.

This was easier said than done on a wriggly little dog who didn't appreciate that we were helping him.

The fur was matted and very red and sticky, and it smelt rather funny, almost fruity. I cleaned the area a little more thoroughly. Could it be, surely not, but yes, it was! A boiled sweet was stuck to Jack's foot, firmly embedded in all the matted hair between his toes!

Eric was a very relieved and slightly embarrassed owner accompanied by jaunty Jack, who felt considerably more comfortable when he left the surgery that day than when he had arrived.

House visits to parrots were not an everyday occurrence in our schedule, so the day an elderly lady who lived in a historic cottage in a picture postcard Peak District village asked me to go and visit her parrot Polly was a memorable one. Emily and Polly had been together for many years, and the two had a mutual understanding. Polly would come out of her cage every morning and fly around the small kitchen and living room behaving herself as long as Emily shared her breakfast with her. Polly loved to eat the corner of a slice of toast and marmalade. If Emily forgot the titbit, Polly would become annoyed, squawk loudly and refuse to go back in her cage. You didn't really want to upset Polly, especially in such a small room.

Most of the time, Polly was a good companion for Emily, and probably vice versa. Emily loved needlework and had embroidered many Peak District scenes, which were framed and hanging in her cottage. They depicted colourful and vibrant flower meadows, cottage gardens in full bloom, and several showed scenes from the annual village Well Dressing tradition. Polly would perch on the back of the armchair while Emily chose the coloured wool for her picture. Sometimes Polly would jump down, pick up a particular-coloured skein of wool and put it in Emily's lap to aid her colour choice.

A few weeks prior to my visit, Polly's behaviour had started to change; she had become angry and, at times, aggressive. Emily was becoming a little scared of Polly but didn't want to keep her shut in the cage all day. What could be wrong with her friend?

Imagine if you will a small, stone, terraced cottage. As you enter the front door, you find yourself in a narrow hallway with a staircase to the upper floor. To the right of the hall is a door through to the modest living room, which in turn leads to the kitchen.

As I entered the dimly lit living room, I was surprised to see an elderly woman wearing a shiny black motorcycle helmet with visor down as she sat in her armchair. This was Emily. She was working on a tapestry (bluebells in a wood). As her needle flew back and forward through the cloth, a grey parrot swooped down and viciously pecked her helmet. On the small table beside her was a piece of toast and marmalade with the corner torn off.

I was temporarily lost for words.

"I have to wear this, or she will peck and wound my head. I've already been to A & E once a couple of weeks ago," said Emily by way of explanation for the surreal scene.

Before further ado, I asked if Polly could be put back in the cage. This took rather a long time to achieve and involved a lot of flying back and forth and angry squawks. Emily and I talked for a while, trying to work out what had changed in Emily's life that could have affected Polly's feelings and, therefore, her behaviour. We decided this was one for the experts; I would find a parrot behaviour expert and refer this case.

I would love to write that all was resolved and ended happily ever after, but sadly very soon after my visit, Emily became ill, and I was unable to follow the path of these two remarkable characters.

CHAPTER SEVEN
NEW LIFE

Helping animals to give birth can be one of the most rewarding parts of a vet's job. Bringing new life into the world is joyful and seeing a new mum bond with her baby is wonderful. The mum will begin licking the newborn immediately, and soon the baby puppy or kitten will be crawling around making little squeaking sounds, or the lamb or calf will be wobbling unsteadily on to spindly legs and trying to find the teat for that first drink of milk.

Sometimes births do not go quite as planned, and this can be a sad occasion. The birthing process may be hard, perhaps too hard for the youngster to survive, or the mother may have a problem and become ill.

One of the calls I remember as having a particularly good outcome occurred one night when I was abruptly awoken from my sleep and asked to visit a farmer whose farm was perched on the side of a hill overlooking a pretty village. He had a cow calving that needed help. I knew he would already have the cow inside the barn with buckets of hot water ready, so all I would have to do would be to put on my protective calving gown, soap my hands and arms and feel inside the mother cow. Calves are usually presented with a head, and both front legs stretched out in front of them, so the calf's hooves are either side of the nose. In this case, I could feel a head but only one front leg. I knew it would not be able to be born in this position, so I felt around deep inside the cow and located the other front leg and managed to manoeuvre it into the correct position taking great care to place my hand over the sharp-pointed little hoof to protect the uterus from tearing as I moved the leg. Once in position and with ropes attached to both of the calf's front legs and another rope around the back of the head to keep it in the right position, the farmer and I pulled on the ropes in time with the cow straining, and the calf was born, all wet and glistening onto the straw. We checked it over; it was a healthy heifer calf, just what the farmer had hoped for. After feeling inside mum again to make sure she had no internal damage and double-check there wasn't another calf waiting to come out, we untied her and let her lick her newborn calf. Just then, John's brother Fred came rushing in

"Before you go, there's another cow calving and not getting on with it; she's out in the orchard. Would you help get her in and have a look while you're here?"

Vets are often asked to look at something else 'while you're here', in fact, many's the time that the 'while you're here' takes longer than the original job you were called to.

A calving cow has to be seen to – even in the middle of the night. It was a lovely mild night, dark but not really pitch black, so we could see sufficiently well to find the cow standing amongst the gnarled old apple trees that had stood in the orchard for generations, sufficient light to safely walk her slowly into the yard, so she didn't slip on the stony ground and then into the barn. This calving was another problem presentation which the cow would not have been able to deliver without help. This time as I reached inside her, I could feel there were two legs but no head. This could either be a calf coming backwards or a case of the head and neck twisting round to one side instead of being presented between the two front legs. I soon discovered it was the latter, the legs were indeed front legs, and with a bit of a stretch, I could feel the neck of the calf turned to one side. These can be tricky to reposition, but luck was on my side that night, and soon I had a rope on the head and had turned it, so it was forward-facing again, and the calf was able to be born. Another healthy live calf, it was a good night's work for the cow, for the farming brothers and for the vet; we were all satisfied.

I drove home to catch a few hours' sleep before the day started again. I knew John and Fred wouldn't have time to get any sleep; they would just have time for a cup of tea before they had to start morning milking.

Sometimes calves cannot be born the natural way, even with the vet's help. The calf may be too large for the mother – either the calf is particularly big, or the mother has been accidentally served by a bull when very young and is too small to give birth naturally – or there may be something wrong leading to the mother's birth canal not dilating, or occasionally the calf has not formed properly meaning a normal presentation for birth is impossible. I have assisted with all these different births; luckily most of them are seen only infrequently. One calving stands out in my memory, and once again, it was in the very early hours of the morning; the full moon was high in the sky, bathing the fields in moonlight. It was an amazing sight, casting a luminescent light on the sleeping world. I drove to the farm to find the heifer who was having difficulty calving had been penned in the corner of a large field a short drive from the farm. I drove through the fields in my car, following Robert the farmer who was in his pickup ferrying buckets of clean water for me to use. When the animal you are examining is in the middle of fields and away from the farmyard, it is necessary to transport any water that will be needed and to try not to slop it over the sides of the buckets as you drive over the uneven ground. Luckily Robert had already caught the heifer; she had a halter on and was tied to the fence of a small enclosure in a hidden valley. It was quite a magical setting at 3am under the full moon. I put on my waterproof gown and examined the heifer; the calf was presented normally and didn't feel unusually large. I attached a rope to the calf's head and legs, applied plenty of lubrication to assist the delivery and we began to pull. It was soon obvious to me that we were making no progress. The calf wasn't going to be born naturally, it would have to 'come out the side door' or, in other words, I would have to perform a Caesarean section. Robert was despatched for more warm water and a straw bale to act as a table. While he drove off, I put on my head torch and started to shave the left-hand side of the heifer where I would make the cut. Next, I injected pain relief and antibiotics and local anaesthetic to numb the area and then scrubbed the whole shaved area with surgical scrub. Just as I was finishing the surgical preparation, Robert arrived back with perfect timing. I opened my pack of sterile surgical instruments onto a sterile cloth placed on the straw bale and scrubbed my hands and arms for a final time before making my incision through the skin and the muscle layers. Once I had opened into the heifer's abdomen, I could feel the uterus with the calf inside; I felt for the calf's hind leg and cut into the uterus over the leg. I could then reach inside and pull both hind legs out through the hole in the side of the heifer and ask Robert to pull on them. At this point, the calf is usually delivered, albeit sometimes with a bit of a pull. This time it just wasn't going to come. I made the hole in the skin longer and enlarged the hole in the uterus and we pulled again, slowly and with a lot of effort from us, the calf began to emerge, and then all of a sudden out it came with a giant thud onto the ground. I turned to see what had caused such a struggle. Robert and I were amazed. The calf was perfectly formed apart from having two heads and necks. This was taking place under the full moon in a hidden valley; I had thought earlier it felt surreal, but now I was sure. I turned back to the heifer and closed the hole in her uterus, then sutured the muscles and skin. The operation was complete; the heifer was looking very well and when we untied her, she walked off to graze a mouthful of grass. We lifted the dead, deformed calf onto the back of the pickup for disposal later that day. Robert returned to the farmhouse; I drove back across the fields onto the lane and then home, reflecting on what an unusual vocation being a veterinary surgeon is.

CHAPTER EIGHT

COMMUNITY SPIRIT

I loved the Peak District from the moment I was taken around on a tour with the boss when I was interviewed for the job vacancy.

The sun was shining on that fortunate day, giving a verdancy to the young green grass beginning to grow in the meadows, the brightness of the grass contrasting with the stone walls surrounding the fields, and the old stone barns dotted around the landscape. The dramatic limestone crags towering white against the cloudless blue of the sky. I remember spotting two figures pressed closely to the rock halfway up an impossibly high vertical wall of limestone. I didn't know then that this area is a mecca for rock climbers whose perilous activities would soon seem commonplace as I drove my way through this landscape every day. I was enthusiastic, and I loved the countryside. I wanted to work in a rural practice looking after a wide range of species from pets to horses to dairy cattle and suckler herds to sheep farms and all the rest in between. There would be family farms, large estates with departmental managers, livery yards, competition horses, family cats and dogs, working dogs, hens, pigeons and the occasional pig.

I accepted the job, booked a self-drive van to transport my furniture and all my worldly goods, including a little black cat who had been brought into my previous practice with three tiny kittens, mewing balls of black fluff looking for a new home. One day I remember sitting in an armchair relaxed with shoes off, legs folded under me while I chatted on the phone; I looked down and curled up inside my sheepskin slipper was a tiny black ball of fluff. He grew up into a handsome black cat much loved by his new owner, one of the veterinary nurses at the practice I worked in at that time. When the kittens were old enough, I found homes for all of them and kept the lovely little black mother cat for many years, a purring affectionate friend.

A bundle of fluff in my slipper

The removal day when I was to begin a new life in Derbyshire dawned grey and overcast. I had only just managed to cram all my furniture, pots and pans, numerous books, many large leggy pot plants and all my other worldly possessions into the white rental van. I pulled down the rear roller door, closing it with a padlock. I had only been to the village where I was to be living on one previous occasion when my new boss had shown me the small cottage which would be my first Derbyshire home. I remembered the cottage was at the very top of a steep, narrow lane winding up from the village main street.

As I approached the village, the sky became greyer, and the light grew darker, then the heavens opened, and the rain began to lash down relentlessly. I turned the headlights to full, put the windscreen wipers to 'fast' and tried to quieten the butterflies in my stomach. I drove along the village main street and indicated to turn up the very narrow lane that would wind through a patchwork of stone cottages sitting close beside one another, each with views out across the rooftops to the hills beyond.

I hadn't recalled how narrow the lane was or remembered the right angle bend I needed to negotiate halfway up the hill. The van only just passed between the stone walls without scraping either side. The torrent pouring from the sky continued. I fervently hoped I had latched the padlock on the rear door effectively; if the door opened unbidden on this hill, my furniture would be deposited in a wet heap in the middle of the road. At best, the contents of the van would have shifted backwards; the carefully nurtured plants would have fallen over, spilling the earth from the heavy crock pots which would have smashed on the floor of the van. The settee would have moved back against the boxes of crockery; it would be mayhem. Eventually, after climbing to a great height, I arrived beside the cottage, my cottage, looking rather grim and grey in the rain.

I parked directly outside the cottage, completely blocking the lane. I unloaded the entire van in the downpour, before the sky cleared and the rain stopped. The van door hadn't opened prematurely, the contents of the van hadn't been squashed and damaged beyond recognition, I only had to move the van up to the wider area of common land above the cottage once to let another car through; what had I been worrying about?

I was both excited and nervous to be starting a new job in a new area where I didn't know a soul. Working within a small rural community, I quickly began to settle in, to learn my way around and establish a routine, or a routine of sorts for every day in the life of a rural vet throws up different challenges and joys. Work is time and energy-consuming; I loved getting to know and to trust both colleagues and clients alike. In those days, I was an assistant at the veterinary practice, but later a colleague and I had the opportunity to purchase the business, and I experienced life on the other side, employing our own team and building new and larger premises.

A vet's life is centred around the animals which need looking after both to prevent illness as well as treating any sickness or injury; it is also centred around the people with whom you work, your colleagues in the surgery, the pet owners, the horse owners and the farmers. I quickly learnt that I had fallen on my feet in the Peak District. People were friendly and helpful and down to earth; they called a spade a spade.

Each village had a real sense of community; people knew each other, knew what was going on and helped each other out when times were tough. In some of the smaller communities, almost the entire population was related, and even in the larger villages, people complained of still being thought of as an 'incomer' even though they had lived there for twenty years or more.

M ost pubs look inviting from the outside and entice you to walk inside to sample their fare and soak up the atmosphere. There is one austere stone building standing at a windswept crossroads, which defies its existence as a pub. The door is always closed; when I went there, I wondered if I had found the right building. Should I knock? Should I walk straight in? I wasn't sure what would be the best approach, so I plumped for the latter and went straight in. The room I entered was small and dimly lit, there was a bar at one end with two torn and dirty armchairs against the wall, in one of which sat a taciturn, hirsute man in patched working clothes, at his feet lay a lurcher dog; resting against the wall was a gun. I hesitated, unsure whether to carry on into the room or retreat into the howling gale outside. The man jerked his head toward a door in the opposite wall

"It's in there", he grunted. No smile of greeting or warming words of welcome issued from his mouth.

Once I opened the door into the next room, I was immediately transported; I was in a crowded room, rough wooden tables filled the floor, and bench seats lined the walls, people were eating homemade rustic food from rustic plates and bowls, enjoying pints of real ale or cider, there was bustle and laughter, warmth and song. People strummed guitars, someone played a flute, and another sang, someone else recited poetry; a scruffy dog sat on one of the benches squeezed between musicians and walkers. Some kind person noticed me looking unsure what to do and moved along to give me room to squeeze onto the bench and order a steaming bowl of homemade soup. I felt extremely glad I hadn't been put off by the outward appearance of this unusual place because in here it was warm and welcoming and full of cheer.

One of the villages I loved to visit as part of my daily work could be approached either by the shorter route, which involved driving through a ford where the stream flowed across the road or by a considerably longer but less hazardous route not involving any water at all. The ford was picturesque with an old wooden footbridge also crossing the stream; the lane dipped down to the ford from one side then wound up the hill between unfenced fields of buttercups and contented black and white dairy cows grazing the rich grass or lying down ruminating and digesting their breakfast. Beneath the water of the ford, the road was cobbled and slippery. Beside the stream, the grassy riverbanks formed an ideal place to spread a plaid rug and sit and drink in the heady scents of summer flowers, listen to the babbling brook and watch the cars negotiate the water. Because of the direction of the fast-flowing water, driving through in one direction seemed much less hazardous than in the other direction. Locals would know not to drive across when the water was deep, but visitors were less wary and could sometimes be observed coming to a spluttering halt in the middle of the stream as water found its way into the engine. They would have to get out of their car in their bare feet, having removed their socks and shoes with difficulty inside the car, they could be watched (or helped) as they tried to get a grip on the slippery cobbles and pushed their vehicle to the other side. It is a lovely spot to sit and tarry a while but preferably not with wet feet or a car stuck in the water while you wait for it to dry out.

Community spirit in the small towns and villages is enhanced by the social activities which take place during carnival or Wakes week. Originally a religious celebration or feast, the tradition of Wakes week developed into a secular holiday during the Industrial Revolution. The village where I lived held events every evening during the week culminating in a stall market at the weekend with traditional Morris dancing in the main street featuring the local team plus a guest team. The Morris team wear white shirts decorated with brightly coloured ribbons, flower-covered straw hats or hair decorations and shoes with bells. There are several accompanying characters, such as the witch, king and queen, all dressed in character costumes. The musicians lead the dancing and call the tune.

No one can be sure of the origins of Morris Dancing. The earliest references, dating from around 1500, are to royal entertainments, but we know that by 1700 Morris dancing had become a firmly established part of English life. Today there are well-known traditional Morris dance teams in the Cotswolds, the Welsh borders and in the north-west, where the Morris is often danced in clogs. The earliest known reference to the Morris in Derbyshire is from the village of Tideswell in 1797. The first mention of Morris in the village of Winster dates from 1863, by which time we know that it was well-established in the village. (https://www.winstermorrisdancers.org/)

One of the other events in Wakes week would be a pet show which I was lucky enough to be invited to judge; I also remember the fell runners' race, a rather hazardous wheelbarrow race in which one person pushed another in a wheelbarrow up one steep village street before descending an equally steep one, a talent show and a pub quiz or perhaps a treasure hunt.

In recent years many of the local villages have opened their private gardens over a weekend for visitors to walk around and admire the flowers and vegetables. There are cream teas to buy, local artwork to enjoy, second-hand bookstalls to peruse or plant cuttings to root through. This is a time to share this wonderful area, to let others see the views from the back of the cottages, to surprise the visitor with the quirky corners of your garden, your horticultural skills and of course to provide refreshments, usually a wonderful selection of cakes made by the villagers served with a freshly made pot of tea.

Lots of villages practise 'Well Dressing', a tradition of blessing the water supply. Wonderful designs made from locally collected flora stuck into clay on a large wooden board are erected over the old water sources, springs or wells. Well Dressings are held in the summer, the themes and pictures depicted on the wells are designed by the villagers, the petals, berries, seeds and whatever else is used to make the picture are collected by the villagers. Clay is soaked or 'puddled' in a local stream or ford and used to cover the wooden boards, and the designs are stuck onto the clay. The designs are displayed for a week, then taken down, painstakingly dismantled, and the frames, boards and clay stowed away for use the following year. The Well Dressings attract lots of visitors and are a major fund-raising opportunity, frequently augmented by local produce stalls, tea shops selling home-baked cakes, cream scones and pots of tea.

I was amazed when I first saw the intricacy of some of the designs. Many tell a story, some are religious, some have contemporary themes, some are crafted by local children, others by artists in the village, all are wonderful to admire. I loved driving through the villages to look at the wells.

I was lucky to find myself living in a vibrant local community and soon felt accepted into its heart. Working as a rural vet enabled me to become acquainted with a lot of people in a comparatively short space of time. I loved the differing characters and personalities I met and with whom I worked.

Derbyshire boasts many stone circles; some are well known and attract many visitors, others are forgotten and only visited by those who know where to look. Stone circles are monuments consisting of a small or larger number of stones placed on the ground at intervals to enclose an area that is often circular. The stones forming a circle are usually approximately equal sizes, but this size varies enormously between circles. These monuments were built in Derbyshire during the late Neolithic and early Bronze Ages, approximately between 3,000 - 1,500 BCE. The reason behind stone circles is not altogether clear though it is thought most had a religious purpose.

One such circle is Nine Ladies Stone Circle on Stanton Moor; the nine ladies form a circle ten metres in diameter. Each stone is less than one metre high. An outlying stone called the 'King Stone', stands away from the circle. Legend has it that one Sunday, nine ladies and a fiddler came up to the moor to dance and for this act of sacrilege, they were all turned to stone.

Another stone circle, Arbor Low, sits on elevated land and is surrounded by a bank and ditch. It is very atmospheric, particularly when the sky is grey and clouds scud along blown by the wind, which is always strong atop this hill.

(http://www.derbyshireuk.net/stonecircles.html)

Chapter Nine
Early morning excitement

An emergency condition that requires attending the farm as quickly as one can is a condition known as 'Milk Fever', which causes muscle weakness and may result in the cow rapidly becoming weak and unable to stand with the possibility of being found lying flat out on her side, often out in the field.

The cow will most likely have become wobbly and staggered about, trying to retain her balance before collapsing. This means that when the vet arrives the cow may not be in the easiest location for the vet to treat her.

Visits to treat cows with milk fever often occur at the beginning or end of the day, and to reach the recumbent cow frequently entails a lift in the farm Land Rover accompanied by one or more collie dogs, or a more perilous ride perched on the side of an ATV or 'quad bike' clutching my medical box containing any equipment I think I will need. Cows are often discovered during the early morning pre-breakfast stock check, coinciding with morning milking, so I have many memories of speeding across hillsides at dawn, descending into deep stony dales, heart in mouth as we lurch from one side of the rutted track to the other with the car at a seemingly impossible angle. Early morning can be a good time for seeing wildlife trotting across the meadows; I loved catching a glimpse of a hare bounding through the grass or watching alert and motionless while we passed by.

I remember a trip to examine one poor cow who had finally 'gone down' in a stream after staggering around the hilly field on her unsteady limbs before they became too weak to support her. Often the cow will have just calved, and she will be lying flat out and unresponsive while her calf stares in bewilderment at its mum. Sometimes the calf will have wandered off and will need to be searched for; perhaps it is lying down behind a bush and can't be seen, let's hope it hasn't wandered into the stream too.

Milk Fever is a shortage of available calcium in the cow's blood. It is one of the conditions which if treated quickly, can lead to such a rapid and dramatic recovery it can seem miraculous. After injecting a bottle of medication directly into the vein, the cow can be transformed from lying flat out on her side not knowing what is going on around her, to sitting up and looking around for her calf within minutes and standing not long afterwards. This is the best result for everyone and very satisfying to witness, particularly if you are lucky enough as you return up the isolated hillside to the farm to see a bushy-tailed fox on his early morning walk through the fields or glimpse a cock pheasant with his spectacular plumage.

a handsome cock pheasant

CHAPTER TEN

A VET'S LIFE IS NEVER DULL

The Derbyshire Peak District comprises limestone dales, rolling pastureland, gritstone edges and moorland. In the limestone area rich mineral deposits lie within the ground, especially lead ore (galena) which has been mined since the Roman times. Many of the stone villages in the valleys or on the hillsides grew up around the mines. The larger houses belonged to the merchants and the maze of tiny houses, reached by winding, narrow footpaths known locally as ginnels are where the miners and their families lived. The very largest houses in the area were built by families who made their fortunes from the lead industry.

Thousands of disused mine shafts; small grass-covered spoil hills or hillocks and ruined buildings are dotted throughout the limestone landscape. Many of the derelict buildings are now little more than piles of stones, some of the shafts have been covered over with old railway sleepers or concrete posts but some are still open, frequently partially covered by grass grown in from the edges lulling the cattle or sheep that live in these fields into a false sense of security.

One of the great things about being a vet in a rural area is that no two days are the same; you never know what you are going to deal with next. In my early days of working in Derbyshire, this sort of terrain and the diseases and occurrences that went alongside it were new to me, but over a few months many would become all too familiar. I experienced very mixed feelings when a call came in one day to attend a bullock that had fallen down an open mineshaft. The farmer was out checking his stock which was grazing on the old 'leaded' area above one of the stone villages when he saw a shaft he didn't recall seeing before. On a closer, and very cautious examination he discovered that what yesterday had looked like a low depression in the grassy field was in fact grass growing from the edge of an open shaft and completely obscuring the shaft and the danger it posed. When the unfortunate beast had walked over this area enjoying munching on the new green grass, the ground had given way beneath its hooves and it had tumbled many feet down into the dank depths of a cylindrical shaft, exactly like falling down a deep, dark well. With much stick prodding on the turf to ascertain the exact edges of the shaft and therefore where would safely bear our weight, and by shining my head torch downwards we could see a large black bullock lodged across the shaft. By large I mean two thirds the size of a fully grown cow. I didn't know how deep this shaft went; the depth miners would have sunk the shaft would have depended on the depth of the lead ore seam they had been working on all those years ago. I didn't think the bullock had reached the bottom of the shaft which could be hundreds of feet deep, it looked as though it was stuck part way, but still a long way down Was it still alive? What if it was alive but not very firmly wedged and it fell further when we were trying to rescue it? Lots of thoughts were racing through my mind as I made tentative plans for each eventuality.

The local fire brigade were 'old hands' at these sorts of calls, they were locals, many had been in the service for several years and had been unfortunate enough to be called out on previous occasions to rescue stock fallen into shafts. I waited with curiosity and a little nervousness for them to arrive. I could see their shiny red engine winding its way along the road towards the village and then being parked at the foot of the hill. The farmer and I waited while the fire crew walked the half mile up the hill to where we were waiting. They had carried all the equipment they would need to erect a tripod over the shaft on which to attach a rope and winding gear to lower the vet down the shaft to examine the beast and then to bring the vet back up to the surface again. You can see why I felt a little anxious.

This called for logical thinking. I would need a torch to see the beast and may need sedative to inject; if the beast was alive, it would need sedating before we tried to attach ropes to pull it back up to the surface. I remember feeling many emotions not least trepidation, but this was accompanied by incredulity and amazement. Once you

embark on the job at hand you concentrate on that task
and all other thoughts diminish.

The firemen strapped me into a harness, gave me a
hard hat and after safety checks started to lower me slowly
into the dark, murky depths. When I was tens of feet into
the earth inside a cylindrical stone shaft and dangling
above the poor beast it was clear that it wasn't moving at
all. I was able to get close enough to ascertain without
doubt that there was no life left. The poor beast, what a
way to die. I signalled to the fire crew to winch me up and
returned to the sunny surface and took a deep breath of
clean air. What a contrast to the darkness and confinement
that had taken this animal's life and had been the daily
workplace for so many men. I know a sadness ran through
me as my feet reached terra firma once more.

M any pasture fields and grazing areas are set
amongst the old hillocks or lead spoil heaps.
These heaps are close to the mine shafts and comprise

excavated soil and rock. A bit like gigantic molehills formed when the mole burrows and displaces earth which is thrown up into mounds on the surface.

Small quantities of lead ore are still found in the soil surrounding these old mine workings. When animals graze, they can ingest small particles of soil stuck to the grass. Young animals are energetic and curious. Little lambs love gathering in groups of five or even ten or more and racing around the field in sheer joy. They jump and gambol; they run up hillocks, standing on the top, playing king of the castle. They wag their tails and jump with all four feet off the ground at once; they investigate anything that looks interesting. Small pieces of rock need mouthing to see what they are; rabbit warrens need investigating to check out who can be seen down the hole. Calves suck their mother's milk and then fancy nibbling at a bit of grass for dessert. Maintenance work can expose soil; I am thinking of the time a large patch of dry soil was newly exposed in the centre of a grazing field by people in fluorescent jackets erecting a new telegraph pole. They would have been blissfully unaware that tiny particles of lead ore were also being exposed as the earth was dug and the grass cover stripped away, leaving curious calves investigating the newly dug earth at risk of suffering the consequences.

Lead is poisonous when eaten; the more that is eaten, the more serious the consequences to the animal. Small, lighter weight animals need to take in only a small quantity of lead before they show signs of toxicity which means young animals run a much higher risk of being poisoned than do fully grown adults. Adults too can be poisoned, and this is not rare in an area such as this one where lead mining was widespread. Of course, farmers learn the high-risk areas and take lots of precautions to protect their stock, but unplanned for events can always catch people out.

Sadly, I soon became familiar with the clinical signs of lead poisoning in cattle and sheep, mainly lambs. Administering treatment fast is crucially important. If an animal does not get treated as soon as possible, it will probably die. One of the first signs you often notice is the animal goes blind. This may sound a very obvious sign, but if you have an animal in the field where usual behaviour includes significant time spent lying down or standing ruminating, being blind or partially sighted isn't always that easy to detect. I came to recognize that animals that cannot see often hold their head at a slightly different angle from those that can see clearly. With lead poisoning, the animal could sometimes become very dopey, but much more usually they would start to twitch and become very excitable if you tried to handle them. This makes trying to treat an animal with lead poisoning a potentially difficult and dangerous task. Within a short time, many affected animals will start to fit or seizure. They will lie flat out on their side with their head back and their legs paddling wildly. Being called out to maybe two or three animals in this sort of distress on a dark night in a muddy field or poorly lit barn is not the sort of call you want to hear when you answer the phone. But, after struggling with sedatives and special intravenous injections, if you save these cows, it is well worth the struggle. Many of our farmer clients became experts at spotting the very early signs of lead poisoning in their stock and would ring us in sufficiently good time for there to be a high success rate with treatment.

One notable Sunday afternoon in mid-winter sticks in my mind. It was a dull and dismal day when the phone rang.

"There's two cows in the cubicles as can't see owt and one them's big calves is thrashing around on the floor. Can you come quick?"

I needed no second bidding. My heart had sunk; this was urgent. I knew this farmer had recently gone out of milk production and now had suckler calves. If a calf died, in addition to the emotional loss for the farmer, there would be no money to be earned from the cow until she calved again in one year's time.

A sorry sight presented itself when I arrived in the farmyard. There was indeed a well-grown calf thrashing around on its side at one end of the large shed, the dirty end. The calf was covered in dirt and muck, which its thrashing legs were spraying over itself and anything nearby. I knew we had to get close enough to the calf to try to quieten it down, examine and treat it. I would need to sedate it as soon as possible and then to inject directly into the vein. Could I do this while avoiding the powerful kicking of the legs? Between us, the farmer and I managed to get a halter on the beast's head, and eventually, the injections were administered, and the calf became less agitated. I was able to turn my attention to the two cows that were blind, not able to see, but not yet in a state of seizure. I was sure these were symptoms due to lead poisoning, but I was perplexed as to where the lead would have come from as none of the stock was outside. The cattle had all been housed inside the big shed for several weeks now and fed only silage. They hadn't been outside grazing, so they couldn't have picked up lead from the fields. Sometimes old vehicle batteries which contain lead are chucked away in far-flung corners of a farm or even thrown into a field by the fly-tipping public. Forgotten or never known about, they rot and pose a real threat to livestock.

By now, the day had advanced, and dusk was upon us. The light in the shed was far from good. A bright and trusty head torch is essential equipment for a rural vet. We searched the shed to no avail; we found nothing that could be a source of lead for the cattle. I knew that if I didn't find the lead, more and more stock would be at risk leading to a potential catastrophe. Even if we could find and remove the source right now, there may be other cows who had already been poisoned and would soon show symptoms.

The farmer and I talked through the complete feeding and management of the herd. It narrowed the risk down to one very expensive area: silage – the conserved grass fodder being fed to the cattle while they were indoors for the winter and the grass in the fields had stopped growing. We made the decision there and then to stop all access to this load of silage and feed an alternative batch. This would be very costly and would entail purchasing additional feed, but we could not take the chance of more animals becoming ill with a high chance of death.

I took blood samples from the affected animals to send to the laboratory to have them tested for lead. The lead level subsequently proved to be very high. Analysis of the silage showed our theory had been correct. High levels of lead were found in the silage, caused by soil being picked up by the machinery when the grass was cut at the start of the silage making process. There had been an unusually high number of molehills in the fields, these had disturbed the earth, and the mounds were in turn disturbed by the mower blades causing soil contamination of the silage crop. Next year the mower blades were set higher, leaving some grass on the fields but ensuring a healthy herd of cattle eating the silage that winter.

CHAPTER ELEVEN

WHAT A FEAST

On the left-hand side of the track along which I was driving, the hillside dropped steeply away to the river flowing along the bottom of the valley, in the distance loomed the mighty stone arches of the viaduct that once proudly carried steam trains full of tourists as they admired the wonderful panoramic vistas; now it is dog walkers and cyclists who chatter and pedal along the route of the old railway.

This was my first visit to this particular client; I had located the farm on the map and was hurrying to see a 'calf with pneumonia'. I hadn't reckoned with a stony, single-track unsurfaced road hugging the side of the steepest hill in the area for what seemed like miles. The 1980s were pre-mobile phones or sat-nav, and to be truthful, in this remote area, they frequently have nil reception even now, so whether I kept going along this precipitous path or retraced my steps and tried another route was down to my map reading skills alone. What was clear was that there was absolutely nowhere to turn the car around, I briefly considered a multiple-point-turn, but the track was far too narrow with a steep bank on one side and vertiginous drop on the other. I couldn't see a farm anywhere along this hillside, so I reluctantly came to the conclusion there was only one option left – I put the car into reverse and made my way slowly, so very slowly snaking back around the hillside, avoiding looking down that stomach-clenching drop. It took ages and ages to reverse back along that rutted, bumpy track and gave me a stiff neck looking over my shoulder for so long, but at long last, a road was reached and very thankfully, I made my way to the lonely farm by the other, metalled road route making a mental note to ask which was the main entrance the next time I saw two roads on a map both leading to a farm.

Being a country vet is an excellent way of getting to know your way around the local countryside, of finding every shortcut along narrow lanes, knowing which village shops sell the best homemade cakes and breads or learning the exact spot you can overtake that quarry lorry you have been following for miles. It also gives an opportunity to learn a lot about the local industry, the local customs, the dialect and the colourful characters that form the soul of any rural area.

Our Derbyshire farmers have hearty appetites. One spring morning, I was up with the lark and heading to a cow that had calved in the night and couldn't get to her feet; she was lying flat out on her side. It sounded like a case of milk fever. It was a beautiful morning; the grass was just beginning to grow after a long winter and was looking a vibrant green on the lower fields; yellow cowslips were abundant in the steeply sloping fields below the rocky limestone outcrops on the tops of the hills.

The cow was lying in a stone barn on a deep bed of straw accompanied by her lovely black calf. I examined her carefully. Our patients can't tell us what is wrong with them, but they usually give us clues! We find these clues when

Cowslips

we take a careful history and make a thorough examination. In this case, the cow had a calcium deficiency or milk fever, not uncommon in dairy cows after calving. I was able to give her a solution of calcium salts directly into her vein, and within minutes she responded and was able to get up onto all four legs. Still a little wobbly but looking much brighter than when I arrived. I was invited into the beautiful old stone farmhouse for a cup of tea. Three brothers worked together on the farm, their parents still lived in the farmhouse, and mum did all the cooking. The brothers worked long hours involving heavy work keeping their dairy herd in tip-top condition and maintaining the miles of stone walls around their fields in good order. They were tall and broad and had appetites to match. I was offered tea and homemade cake, which I devoured. I was full of admiration at the size of the breakfasts consumed that morning. Each brother had a large pudding basin full to brimming with four Weetabix or Shredded Wheat covered with fresh creamy milk straight from their milking parlour and a liberal sprinkling of sugar. This was followed by a plateful of traditional English breakfast, bacon, eggs, sausages and tomatoes, followed by rounds of hot buttered toast, all washed down with mugs of tea. Wow, what a feast! My eyes were out on stalks as I bid them goodbye and set off for the surgery to start my day's work.

Chapter Twelve
Feeling bloated

Country folk use country sayings, and in Derbyshire, these very descriptive words and phrases are announced in broad dialect. I became overly familiar one year with a certain descriptive saying used by a farmer when he encountered lots of trouble caused by feeding his fattening bullocks on potatoes. Potatoes can be a valuable food for cattle but are not without risk, especially when the potatoes being offered to the stock are all spherical of a specific size and fed whole rather than broken into smaller pieces beforehand, which is the more usual way of presenting them in feed.

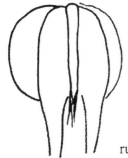

After a cow has chewed and swallowed its food, whether the food is lush fresh spring grass, preserved grass silage, maize silage, corn or potatoes, the food starts to be digested in the very large stomach called the rumen. This results in the production of a large volume of gas which is passed out of the stomach and dispersed when the beast belches. Gas can also pass out the other end too but for this story belching is the important action. Or perhaps, in this case, I should say, not belching is important.

If a beast attempts to eat a certain sized, regular, round potato while it is still too large to pass all the way to the stomach, there is a very high chance it will be swallowed before it has been completely chewed. If it is just too large, it will get stuck. Can you imagine how painful it would be to have a potato, a whole potato, not just a chip, stuck in your gullet? There are multiple other effects too. A cow produces many litres of saliva every day to help chew and digest its food. If the food is stuck, the saliva will be produced but not be able to be swallowed, and the cow will dribble excessively, copiously. The cow will not be able to eat or drink because it cannot swallow. But of even greater immediate importance is the fact that with their oesophagus well and truly blocked, the beast cannot belch. And if the gas cannot readily escape from the stomach, the stomach distends; and continues to distend until the beast looks like a balloon with four spindly legs waiting to take off and fly over the Peak District. The pressure within the rumen will build and build until it presses on the vena cava, the great vein returning blood to the heart. If blood can't return to the heart, the beast will die.

So, when the farmer rings the surgery and says

"I've got a 'tatered beast" you know that he means he has a beast with a potato stuck in its gullet, and you need to get there very swiftly.

The first thing to do is to insert a gag into the beast's mouth to aid examination. A gag is a metal or plastic instrument that is lodged between the upper and lower cheek teeth as a means of keeping the cow's mouth open. A cow's tongue is a massive and very strong muscle. It is very long and coated with slimy saliva, and it has a roughened upper surface to help move food backwards in the mouth. At the very back of the mouth near the throat, the tongue has a large natural lump on it. You have to grasp the tongue tightly in one hand and pull it forwards and sideways while at the same time sliding the metal gag between the upper and lower cheek teeth in the beast's mouth. The teeth are sharp, finger losing sharp, and the jaw is powerful. You have to be exact and work quickly. Once the gag is in place, you are a little safer and can try to deduce where along the gullet the potato is stuck. The gullet is long, and the potato often lodges way past the throat and out of sight. I knew I had to try to propel the potato towards the stomach using a specially designed stiffened tube similar to a hosepipe with a flattened end. Great care must be taken not to push the potato through the side of the gullet, or all, including the beast, will be lost.

On one occasion, when the potato was less than my arm's length down from the mouth, I managed to insert my arm down the beast's throat while at the same time holding a corkscrew (the corkscrew just happened to be in my car in case of such eventualities). I tied it to my wrist so I wouldn't lose it when my fingers were slimy and covered in saliva. Gloves too get very slippery when coated in cattle saliva. With a lot of effort and what could pass for dexterity, I screwed the corkscrew into the potato and pulled the offending object back out through the cow's mouth.

Other causes of 'obstructive bloat' are seen, and when called to such a case it is important to examine the mouth in great detail to determine why the cow is unable to belch or 'eructate', which is the technical term. I remember examining a dairy cow's mouth. This cow was not eating; she was salivating profusely and was a little blown in her stomach. Examining the back of her mouth was not an easy task. Firstly, the handling facilities were not the best, and the ambient light was poor. The cow had a painful throat and did not want a vet examining it, so someone had to keep her head still, then I had to get hold of her tongue, insert a gag and use my trusty head torch to get a really good view of her enormous molar teeth and the back and sides of the tongue. I inserted my hand well above the wrist and was able to feel over the lump at the back of the tongue, and there I found the cause of the problem. The cow's throat was impacted, completely jam-packed with masses of silage which the cow had taken into her mouth, chewed and forced backwards by the motion of the tongue, but something was stopping it from being swallowed. More and more silage had been taken in because the cow was hungry, and it was forming a solid smelly mass in the back of the mouth. With great difficulty, I pulled it out bit by smelly bit until the area was clear. At first, it was a mystery why the impaction had occurred until eventually, when the mouth was clear of food, I could see a large gash on the side of the cow's tongue, right at the back, against the molar teeth. She must have picked up something razor-sharp tangled in the silage, perhaps a shard of rusty metal which had lacerated her tongue and stopped it being able to move sufficiently well to allow her to be able to swallow properly.

A course of treatment and adjusting her diet to include something easier to eat worked well, and she was soon back to the best of health. I took time to thoroughly cleanse myself and my instruments before leaving the farm, but I knew I would be able to smell the saliva and impacted silage for the rest of the day.

You can now understand why, when a farmer says, "I've got a blown cow" "and she's not looking too good", I know I have to hurry. I have to hurry because a blown cow could translate into a dead cow. There's no popping into the corner shop for one of those newly baked tea cakes or perhaps a sausage roll to munch on the way to the call; I won't be tempted to treat myself to a jam doughnut on the way to this call. (Why is it that however careful I am, I always find a spot of bright red jam has silently dropped out of the doughnut and splodged onto my trousers where it sits as glaring evidence for the rest of the day only concealed during farm visits by workmanlike over trousers?).

If the bloat is caused by something other than a blockage in the oesophagus, in order to relieve the cow, it is necessary to let the gas escape directly from the stomach to the outside, but not too quickly, not in one sudden rush, so the cow suddenly deflates like a punctured balloon. The gas must be let out slowly so the cow can cope with the pressure changes inside her body.

When I arrive and tend to the cow, I inject some local anaesthetic into the skin, where it is tightly stretched over the expanded stomach. Then I make a small incision through the tough skin using a surgical blade before inserting a cannula straight through the muscles and into the stomach. The gas wooshes out with gusto, accompanied by flecks of partially digested grass and a very pungent smell. I control the speed of the gas release with my finger. Thank goodness the farmer gave up smoking years ago, for this gas contains methane which is highly flammable. I've heard tales of barns burning down when a spark has caught the expelled air.

Once all the air has come out from the stomach, I secure the cannula in place, making a temporary hole in the side of the cow to ensure she doesn't become bloated again in the next few hours. The cannula can be removed in two days, and the hole will heal by itself.

I leave the farm with the cow comfortable and safe, and the farmer relieved.

CHAPTER THIRTEEN

WILD WEATHER

During the whole of my life, I have always been very influenced by the weather, never more so than when working as a vet in the peaks and dales of Derbyshire. A stressful day can be lightened by a drive through countryside with magnificent views over rolling pastures, alongside wide rivers crossed by ancient stone bridges, or landscapes dominated by majestic gritstone edges.

Being suddenly awoken by the phone, then dragged from your warm bed far too early in the morning is never pleasant, but the rewards are reaped by seeing the sunrise, a yellow orb appearing over the horizon and bathing the fields and woods in bright, new light. Animals and birds not often seen outside the crepuscular hours delight the early riser with glimpses into a secret life. The barn owl flying silently with white wings wide, the now sadly scarce brown hare loping through the ancient pastures thrill me. Deer are widespread in this area, dark brown, almost black fallow deer graze in herds eating the choice grass. They hop over the stone walls with a fluid movement. Driving back home one night on a stretch of road passing through a dark wood, a deer jumped out right in front of my car, causing me to slam on the brakes. Phew, that was a near miss. One very early morning, I came across a tiny fawn standing in the road in a patch of dappled sunlight; it couldn't have been more than a few hours old. I watched as the doe emerged from the trees, nuzzled it before disappearing once more into the woods with the little fawn following.

Foxes would sometimes trot silently across the field or appear crossing an urban road and make their way up a garden to investigate if a meal could be found near the house. Hedgehogs were not an unusual sight moving with amazing speed along the road looking for food and sadly I saw dead ones too, unlucky hedgehogs going about their life then suddenly squashed and killed by a speedy car.

The countryside can be spectacular under a full, shining spherical moon. On one visit at night, the bright moonlight shone on the fields, suffusing them with a bright, clear light bestowing a magical quality to the countryside.

Winter weather influences the pace of the day. Snow is

beautiful to look at; it transforms the countryside in a few short hours into a silent wonderland, obliterates landmarks and changes landscapes and softens contours. But snow makes hard graft of everything connected with work. Making fresh tracks in the snow on a skiing holiday is an amazing and uplifting experience but peeping through your curtains to discover a snowy world at home and recognising you are going to be making fresh tracks down the road in your car is not a nice awakening. My snow shovel, extra clothes, a warm blanket and food rations lived in my car from autumn until late spring. If I should be unfortunate enough to skid off the road, particularly in an area of poor phone reception, I needed to be prepared.

Certain nights are predicted by meteorologists to be very good for seeing shooting stars or meteor showers. Visibility is based on a variety of factors, including weather and astronomical conditions. One late evening I was performing a caesarean section at a hilltop farm on a suckler cow who had not been able to deliver her calf naturally. She was tied by her halter rope to a gate in an open-fronted barn. Throughout the operation, we were treated to a wonderful display of meteors shooting across the sky. Afterwards, when I had put the final suture in the cow's skin and the calf was shakily trying to get to his feet, we humans stood in silence gazing at the dark sky with a myriad of stars and sharp tracks of bright light darting across. It was an amazing experience, one that will stay with me for a very long time.

E lectric storms can be terrifying, especially when thunder crashes overhead and the sky lights up as forks of lightning crackle angrily overhead and discharge their fury on anything in their path. Rain lashes down in stair rods upon the cattle in the fields. They will take shelter under the dense canopy of the sycamore trees or huddle under the ash trees, which dominate the landscape in many of the limestone areas of the peak district.

Imagine my horror when I received a call the morning following a fierce electric storm. A dairy farmer with a fabulous herd of Holstein dairy cows had walked to the field to bring his herd in for morning milking and was confronted by a scene of shattering horror.

Fifteen of his cows were lying on their sides near the tree.

Each one unmoving, unmarked.

Each one dead.

Killed by lightning.

S tock is insured for loss due to a lightning strike, so I was often called out to certify that this was the cause of death. Sometimes a post-mortem examination may need to be carried out to establish the true cause of death. I hardly ever saw any external mark on the carcase indicative of burning, but if the animals were in an exposed position or near a potential electrical conductor and there had been an electric storm at the time of death, circumstantial evidence would be important.

Lightning used to be said to scorch the ground or travel along the ground in straight lines. This assumed great importance when I took a phone call from a farmer one day.

"There's two bullocks dead int' field" "I found 'em this morning when I drove up to check."

"It's lightning what's killed 'em" "Can you do me a certificate?"

"That sounds bad, Jim", I replied down the phone, "Have you had a storm up there in the hills? I don't think we had one down here last night?"

"Oh yes, rained real 'eavy and I 'eard a clap of thunder over yonder."

"What makes you sure the beasts got struck by lightning? It does happen but not too often, thank goodness?"

"Oh, there's no doubt, no doubt at all. There were two of them dead in the same field. They were lying in a straight line they were. One of 'em dead by the wall t'other in t'middle of field, in a straight line, as I said"

I still chuckle when I recall the conversation. Two in a straight line...

Cattle are much more susceptible to electric shocks than most other animals, and they can be electrocuted by causes other than lightning. Dairy cows are milked two or three times every day. At milking times, the herd goes through the milking parlour, where each cow is milked and often receives a small quantity of food.

It was halfway through evening milking one Christmas Eve when I received a call to say that some of the cows in the parlour had been electrocuted and was asked if I could go as quickly as I could. On arrival at the farm, it was a scene of total devastation. Every one of the eight cows on one side of the parlour (there were eight cows on each side of the parlour being milked at the same time) had been electrocuted and dropped down dead in an instant. Some were lying half on top of the one in front; one had fallen down into the pit, which is where the person doing the milking stands surrounded by equipment used to milk the cow and jars for storing the milk before it flows into the bulk tank. One of the cows had fallen on top of the exit gate at the front of the parlour. The eight cows on the other side of the parlour had been spared and were still alive. The farmer said it looked as though all the metal feeders on one side of the parlour had become live and touched every cow on that side. As soon as this happened, the cows were electrocuted and dropped down stone dead.

In the collecting yard, there were sixty or seventy cows, all with full udders. They were becoming uncomfortable waiting to be milked and fed, but they couldn't get into the parlour, which was blocked by dead cows, and all the electricity was turned off until it could be made safe.

The farming family were marvellous in the face of this catastrophe; they remained calm and helpful. Help arrived, and the dead cows were winched out of the parlour and taken away; the electricity supply was checked and repaired. It was several hours and technically already Christmas Day before the rest of the herd could be milked.

Chapter Fourteen
Winter turns to spring

Country vets love springtime. The countryside begins to awaken, buds on the branches start to swell, the grass takes on a bright green hue, and the birds begin to sing at the top of their voices.

The smell of damp grass, the coconut smell of yellow-flowered gorse bushes, the heady perfume of bluebells as they carpet the woods with blue are all magical signs that new life is bursting forth. It makes one glad to be driving around tending to the livestock in this beautiful area. Most lambing happens in late spring around here, starting in April or May, hoping there will be some warm weather and sun to make life easier for the newly born lambs. Often the pregnant sheep are brought inside a few weeks prior to lambing, brought into warm sheds where they can be more easily cared for, and help is at hand if a ewe gets into trouble lambing.

After the lambs have been born, they are penned in a small enclosure alongside their mum, so they bond as a family and mother and young ones will be able to find each other when they are turned out with the rest of the flock to graze in the lush fields

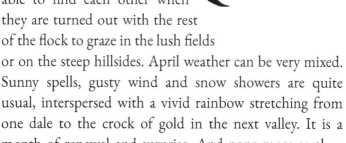

or on the steep hillsides. April weather can be very mixed. Sunny spells, gusty wind and snow showers are quite usual, interspersed with a vivid rainbow stretching from one dale to the crock of gold in the next valley. It is a month of renewal and surprise. And none more so than one night when I was rudely awoken in the early hours by the insistent ring of a phone.

"I've a ewe as can't lamb; she's one of me best. Can you come?"

Ten minutes later, I was on my way. I knew the farm, a family farm at the 'top end' of a small stone village 1000 feet up in the hills. The sheep were Pedigree Suffolks, lovely, big sheep with characteristic black faces and ears.

This was a high-quality flock; the sheep on this farm were very well managed. The farmer was experienced, and if he was unable to help the ewe, it must be an unusual presentation, a very tricky birth. It was a horrible night. The rain was pouring down, leaving big puddles on the roads, I knew the sheep would be housed inside a warm barn, and I was thankful, for them and for me.

On arrival, I collected my lambing kit from the car boot and hurried towards the stone barn, which was lit up and shone like a beacon through the stormy darkness. I battled through the near-horizontal rain and wind toward the welcoming light. Inside was like a haven of peace. It was warm and quiet, just the contented sounds of slumbering sheep and the welcome presence of the farmer, Bill sitting on a straw bale with a bucket of warm water ready for me.

"Hello Bill, what a night. Shall we have a look at her then?"

I could see the ewe, lying in a well-strawed pen, lifting her head every time she strained. I put on my arm length plastic gloves and applied lots of lubricant before feeling inside the warm ewe. I could feel a head and two little hooves. Gently I assessed the size of the head and the size of the mother's pelvis. I knew she would not be able to lamb naturally; this lamb was too big it would have to 'come out the side door.'

"She needs a caesarean, Bill. The lamb's a large one."

We put two straw bales next to one another and lifted the ewe on her side on top. I shaved the fleece from an area on her left flank and scrubbed it up. I changed into a clean smock and opened my pack of sterile operating instruments onto another straw bale 'table' placed where I could reach it but well out of the way of my patient's kicking legs just in case the ewe should struggle. After numbing the area with local anaesthetic and injecting pain relief and antibiotics, I carefully cut through the skin and muscle to get inside the abdomen. I put my arm inside and felt the lamb through the wall of the uterus. I cut over the lamb's back leg and pulled it out from the uterus and out through the side of the ewe, and laid it onto the straw. Bill checked it over, cleaned its mouth and nostrils of mucus and made sure it was breathing strongly. Lambs usually sit up and shake their heads almost immediately after they are born; this is a good sign that they are strong and have not suffered ill effects coming into this world. Thankfully this was a strong and healthy lamb. I quickly sewed up the uterus and muscle and skin, cleaned the ewe and stood her up on her feet. She was eager to lick her lamb, which by this time was on his feet and wobbling around looking for somewhere to suckle.

It was a lovely timeless scene. The ewe and lamb were well, Bill, the farmer, was satisfied, I was happy, and there was still time to get home and snatch a couple of hours sleep before the 'proper' day began. But I was reluctant to leave the peace and warmth of the barn, to leave the mums and their lambs and the very pregnant ewes who were still not ready to lamb. But leave, I must. I pushed open the barn door to go to my car and could hardly believe my eyes. The world was transformed. Where before there was hammering rain and howling wind, there was a silent

white world. It was snowing; the flakes were large and
fluffy and had settled on everything. It was several inches
deep and still falling in bucketsful from the sky. The yard
was covered, the lane was covered, but my car was a four-
wheel drive, and I hoped fervently it would cope. I
gingerly started home, I had never realised before, in better
conditions, how steep the road through this village
actually was, and now I was going downhill in the dark in
a snowstorm, on a road so covered in snow that I could
barely see it I realised too late that I wasn't going along a
horizontal road but was heading down a pretty steep hill. I
gently braked. I wasn't going as slowly as I had thought;
my tyres were on the verge, or where I thought the verge
was under all the snow, and then I was sliding across the
road, and then the wheels were on the other verge. I was
gripping the steering wheel and trying to stay calm, but I
knew there was a sharper bend fast approaching, then a
really steep downhill section before meeting a T junction
with a stone wall on the far side of the T of the junction. I
had once been on a fun day out on a skid pan, and I put all
I had learnt into practice. I slid from one side of the road
to the other; I slid around the bend and gathered speed
down the hill. What could I do? At least I knew there was
little chance of meeting another car on such a night deep
in the country at 4am. I shot down the hill straight across
the T junction and into the snow-covered grass bank atop
of which was a dry-stone wall; I had finally come to a stop.
The wall was not damaged, I was not damaged, no one else
was involved; I hoped the car was OK too.

Gingerly I engaged reverse gear and backed away from

the bank, changed up to first gear and carried on down the hill crawling along in first gear, keeping my foot well away from accelerator and brake. Imagine my astonishment when after 50 metres of descent, the snow turned to rain, heavy rain but not a sign of snow, not one flake anywhere. I could scarcely believe the difference the altitude had made.

I reached home, went to bed and tried to get some sleep before the morning's work started. I must have just lapsed into slumber when the alarm shattered my dreams. I crawled out of bed and looked out of the window; the world was wet and grey. Had I been dreaming, or had I really had a surreal snowy experience while the world slept?

Cautiously I walked out to my car; all was as it should be except for several huge clods of earth firmly stuck in the front bumper. I knew then I hadn't been dreaming.

CHAPTER FIFTEEN

ADVERSE CONDITIONS

There is a saying by visitors from the South of England that 'you need to wear an extra coat in Derbyshire'. My first winter in the area came as a shock. My cosy stone cottage was at the top of a steep, narrow lane that wound its way up through the village. When you wake in the morning and look out onto a white and silent wonderland, at first it's beautiful, but in an instant, the practicalities kick in. Four-wheel drive cars have revolutionised the ability of a farm vet to get to calls, the cars are able to go up steep stony farm tracks, they can traverse muddy fields to reach cows stranded miles from farm buildings, and they are even good in snow, except when you go too fast downhill as you have heard. Even with a 4WD car, you are thwarted when you walk outside and find the snow has blown into the lane from everywhere around, has filled the space created by the dry-stone walls bordering the lane, has blown down from the hill above the cottage and still keeps falling in big, white flakes. On this particular morning, my car bonnet was covered. I don't mean covered only because the snow was falling on it from above. It was covered because the depth of snow was high enough from the ground to cover the bonnet.

I knew it was no good taking out my trusty snow shovel, which lived permanently in the car. This was far more than my shovel could cope with. This depth of snow wasn't a single mound where the wind had blown; this depth of whiteness stretched all the way up the lane and into the distance. This is when my phone rang.

Oh heck, a ewe needing help to deliver her lamb, how on earth was I going to get there? Luckily the farm was quite close by, and the farmer offered to come and pick me up on the tractor; we would never get there any other way. I had to think carefully of all eventualities and pack everything I might need into a bucket that I could take with me on the tractor. It was an exciting way to get to a lambing. High up on a huge tractor, easily making its way through the snowy landscape. The ewe was having twins which were both trying to come out together. I could feel a head and two front legs, but both legs didn't belong to the same lamb. I managed to find the leg which belonged to the lamb whose head and leg were already presented and delivered the first lamb. The second soon followed. We left the mum licking two lovely, lively lambs and, after washing myself down, went inside for a cup of tea before climbing back onto the tractor and being driven back to my house.

Another time I remember being called out to a farm one snowy evening and getting stuck in a snowdrift in the darkness on my way home. When snow lies on the roads and the wind is blowing, you find that most roads can be passable in most places, but where there's a gap in the dry stone walls on either side of the road or where there is a gateway in the wall, the wind blows through, and the snow drifts across the road causing a real hazard. When it's blustery and the snow is swirling in the air, it can be very hard to determine where the snow is drifting and lying thickly on the ground or where it is passable by car. I had driven into one such drift where I had miscalculated the depth of snow on the road, and the car soon came to a full stop. I got out of my car into the swirling wind, put on my trusty head torch over my woolly hat, retrieved my snow shovel from its place behind the front seats and started to dig. After a while, I could see digging was futile. I was not making any headway and was expending a huge amount of effort. The snow was very tightly packed under the car where I had driven into the drift. I would never shift it. So, I locked the car (not that anyone else was mad enough to be out here on this country road in the dark in driving snow) and set off to walk to the nearest farm. Luckily it wasn't too far, and I knew the farming family who welcomed me with a mug of tea before giving me a lift on their tractor back to my car, then attaching a rope to the car and towing it out of the drift and back to the road already cleared by snowplough so I could drive back home.

Aged 19, taking a prize-winning Hereford bull
for his morning exercise.

Relaxing in my garden,
1990s.

The little black cat who came with me to Derbyshire, 1992.

Enjoying a sunny walk, 2011.

Visiting Highfield House farm, pictured in 2022.

Many thanks to the Prince family for allowing us to visit and take pictures

Chapter Sixteen
An Unknown Diver

Dairy cows usually behave themselves when they are out in a lush green pasture with lots of long verdant grass to munch. They are quiet and well-mannered, roaming around in a group, then lying and ruminating as they digest the food which will produce many litres of nutritious milk every single day of their lactation.

The fields of the Peak District often contain a 'mere' or man-made pond, usually circular constructed in days of old as watering holes for the cattle. These meres are shallow and allow safe access to the water for the cattle to drink. However, if the pasture field happens to contain a large, muddy lake that has been fenced off for years because it is dangerous being boggy around the edges and deep in the middle, and if the cows one day discover a hole in the fencing and go to investigate, it can be a very different story.

One of the more unusual and quite alarming calls I

received was from a farmer who was very worried because one of his heifers had somehow gained access to the lake and was standing nearly submerged in the centre. Every time she moved, the mud would slowly but surely gain an increasingly strong grip on her legs, and she was gradually disappearing into the muddy morass.

On arrival at the farm, I saw I wasn't the only rescue service on hand; the fire brigade was in attendance too. They were easily recognisable in their bright yellow gear and yellow helmets, but I didn't recognise the person in the black wetsuit trying to walk through the energy-sapping boggy ground surrounding the lake. At least I didn't recognise him until he spoke, and then the light dawned. He was not a professional rescuer wearing a wet suit but was, in fact, my farmer friend John covered from head to toe in black slime! He had struggled, part wading, part swimming into the lake to try to help his heifer get back to firm ground before she gave up her struggle to swim, and then to live.

The water was deep, the mud was even deeper, the heifer could neither stand still and defeat the pull of the mud, nor keep trying to swim. She was heavy in calf and would soon tire if she wasn't pulled out onto dry land. I had to come up with a plan to save her life and the life of her unborn calf.

The farmer wouldn't give up his fight to rescue his heifer; he insisted that he wanted to go back into the lake to try to position a sling around the heifer's belly. This meant he had to reach down into the mud to pass the sling far enough underneath the heifer so that he was able to grab hold of it on her other side. Somehow, after what seemed like a very long time, John managed to position the rope and then we managed to put a halter on her. With the halter rope and sling attached to the front loader of a tractor, she could be raised up out of the foul-smelling black liquid and deposited on the grass. This is easy to write but lengthy and nail-biting to witness. When eventually she was back on dry land and safe, we hosed her down, and probably hosed the farmer down too, but I can't quite recall that fact! The heifer was given water to drink, then was dried by rubbing her vigorously with some straw before turning her into a barn with some others from her group. Cattle are social creatures and feel less stressed if they are with their cohorts.

I was the first to drive away from the farm, leaving the fire brigade to stow their equipment and follow me down the narrow lane in their large fire engine. It was several days later and many showers and changes of clothes before I finally managed to get rid of the fetid smell.

A few days later, Helen, the farmer's wife, came into the surgery with the delightful news that the heifer was fine and had calved without assistance and now had a lovely heifer calf of her own. Helen was bearing a small gift for me. It was such a lovely gesture, one I didn't feel I deserved but was much appreciated. I had to laugh when I opened the gift – it was a coffee mug, wholly coloured black to remind me of mud!

CHAPTER SEVENTEEN
HANDLEBAR HORNS

Acow's womb (or uterus) is an internal organ that varies greatly in size depending on whether the cow is not in calf or is just about to produce a 40Kg robust youngster. As a vet, I am well acquainted with both states. A lot of my time was spent with my hand 'up the backside' of a cow or, to be more technical, per rectum, allowing me to palpate the uterus and ovaries. In my hand would be an ultrasound scanner to enable the ovaries and uterus to be visualised, thus enabling reproductive problems to be corrected and early pregnancies detected. Dairy cows produce milk, but only in response to producing a calf, so to produce milk, the cow has to become pregnant and calve down nine months later. Many is the morning when I would arrive at the farm to be greeted by a group of cows who had been separated from the herd, waiting to file into the parlour or crush one at a time for me to examine their reproductive tract or stage of pregnancy. This type of herd health visit confers many management and financial advantages for the farmer, but there are additional and more prosaic problems for the vet: you soon develop well-muscled arms; I have even been asked if I was a rock climber! You 'wear' a perfume which hasn't cost a fortune but is 'earthy with a hint of grass' (or perhaps clingy with more than a hint of farmyard?). On cold days when the frost is creeping into the corners of the building, and the wind is roaring through the passageways, this job keeps your hands warm. You wear (rather fetching) shoulder-length disposable gloves which you cover in lubricating gel. You immerse your hand and arm inside the cow, if you are small in stature, your face is rather too close to the cow's backside, which explains why I often had a green-brown smudge on my chin. Your hand is in the warmest place possible, it may be messy and smelly, but at least it's warm.

When the cow is ready to calve, the uterus has expanded to hold the calf and all the fluid surrounding the calf. When I assist the cow to calve, I am very careful to protect the inside of the uterus as I reposition the calf by moving its head or limbs into a more manageable position or when I put a rope on the head or on the limbs to aid delivery. When the calf is unable to be delivered in the normal way, I may need to perform a caesarean section. Then after I have cut through the skin and muscle on the side of the cow, I can actually see the uterus inside the cow. I can feel the calf through the uterine wall, but it isn't until I cut into the uterus that I can see and directly feel the calf. Once I have cut into the uterus and removed the calf through the hole, it is amazing how quickly the uterus starts to shrink in size and how small it becomes. I have carried out caesarean sections on various cattle in many varied conditions and many different times of the day and night. I have a few special memories; unsurprisingly, many seem to be at the weekend or during the evening or night.

One memory is of a mid-winter's evening call to a beef farm. The farmer didn't have a lot of stock; his beef cows were housed in very clean sheds, and the facilities for the stock and for the vet were good. My main memory is of the cold that night. You could see your breath in front of you in icy blasts. I remember thinking not many surgeons count a woolly hat as part of their operating clothes. It was one of the quickest operations I have ever done. My hands were warm when they were inside the cow, feeling the calf and cutting through the uterus. But as soon as I was suturing the cow from the outside, my hands were frozen. I quickly realised if my hands were so cold that they were numb it would be very hard to stitch up a cow. This was a good incentive, and a fine live calf had been delivered in record time and was being licked by a happy mum.

Derbyshire is dotted with small stone field barns, which each used to house three or four beasts, the total farm stock in times gone by. Now many of the barns have been left to slowly crumble or have been sold off and converted into houses. Some are still used as a place in which to herd stock when you need to catch them or for shelter for the stock grazing the field. One late weekend evening, I was called to see a heifer belonging to a farmer who only had a few cattle. This heifer was having difficulty calving. She was in a small stone barn across a field off a country lane. I drove over the field to the barn and quickly realised the heifer was too small to deliver the calf naturally, so a caesarean was needed. The light was fading fast outside, and inside the stone barn was almost black. I had my head torch, but, on this occasion, we also had another source of light – on the wide stone windowsill the farmer placed a lighted candle, and I proceeded to perform surgery by candlelight. The heifer behaved impeccably and was soon nuzzling a live calf. I didn't dwell on what might have happened with a lighted candle and a barn floor covered with straw if all hadn't gone to plan.

Another memory is of a cow who was not quite so well behaved. She was unused to being handled and was wild in her behaviour. She was a smallish cow with 'handlebar horns'. These are horns that grow upwards from the head in a wide curve resembling handlebars. I was soon very grateful for these imperfectly shaped horns. When I received the call one late Sunday afternoon to a cow who was having trouble calving and was 'down the fields', I had a premonition I might be in for some fun. I knew from experience the cow on this farm would not be used to being handled and thus may be hard to manage. On arrival, I parked on the side of the lane and carried my calving equipment over the stone wall, then across the field toward the tiny derelict stone barn where the farmer had put the cow. First, we had to catch the cow. This is where an old-fashioned set of horns comes in handy; a rope can be lassoed around the horns and then thrown over the horizontal roof timber – the only thing in the entire barn to which a rope could be attached. The cow proceeded to run round and round in small circles tied by the single rope stretching upwards to the distant roof beam until I managed to inject her with a sedative, and she gradually became quieter and lay down. I sprang into action. After an examination, it was soon apparent to me that the calf was too large to be delivered in the normal way and would need to be delivered by caesarean section. I would have to be quick and work while the patient was still sleepy. I quickly leapt into action to shave and clean the cow. For this, I required water, so I asked farmer Paul for some.

"There's no running water down here."

My heart sank; I couldn't perform fairly major surgery with no water

"There's a trough in this field; I'll get some from that," said Paul, always the optimist.

When the two buckets of water arrived, one looked reasonably clean; the other had green pondweed floating in it. I put my hand into the bucket, removed a good handful of weed and carried on.

There was no makeshift table on which to place the sterile instruments required for performing the surgery. I had to place the sterile drape and the sterile operating instruments onto the baked earth floor. All was going well, and the cow was lying very sleepily. I had removed the perfectly formed live calf and was about to start closing everything up when without warning, the cow jumped up onto her feet and lurched forward.

Somehow, I managed to grab the sterile instruments or those that were not already scattered around the barn, and Paul grabbed the cow by her horns, then held her by her nose to keep her still while I took a deep breath and quickly sutured the wound in her side.

The calf thrived, and the cow went on to make an uneventful recovery. Luck was on my side that day.

Cows vary greatly in size, not only depending on their age but also depending on their breed. Limousin cattle are a large breed of beef cattle; we treated several pedigree Limousin herds. When cows are used to being handled, they can be docile and amenable, and if handling facilities were available on the farm, there would be few problems tending to a sick cow. On some farms, however, the animals were not handled very often and consequently could be wild and troublesome and potentially dangerous, so getting a call to one of these farms where a Limousin was having difficulty calving could be problematic. Before I can examine a cow, she must be restrained. If she is used to being tied with a halter restraining her is easy. If there is a 'crush' available, this is also helpful. If neither of these is available, one of the favourite ways for farmers to restrain the cow is behind a five-barred gate. If the gate is tied at one end to the wall of the pen, the cow can be enticed into the gap between the gate and the wall, then the gate swung across to wedge her tightly. This is not always satisfactory, especially if you are trying to work over or through the bars of the gate. On this farm visit, I had nearly finished a caesarean on a large Limousin cow weighing about 700Kg; there was a live calf already struggling onto his feet. I had completed the internal sutures and was halfway through suturing the skin, the last part of the operation when all of a sudden, with no warning, I was knocked backwards off my feet and, as I fell, was aware of my sterile suture instruments soaring through the air and landing in the straw. Amazingly I was scarcely even winded. How the cow had managed to get her feet up and kick me through the gate as she did, I still don't know, but there was no time for thinking; we had to keep her restrained and finish sewing her up. We got her back into position behind the gate, and I finished the job. Mother and son never looked back. I nursed a bruised arm for some days, and I was very lucky it hadn't been worse. I knew I'd had a lucky escape!

Chapter Eighteen
Llama Alarm

A vet can be presented with many different types and breeds of animals that, between them, will experience a wide variety of illnesses or accidents in diverse settings. You will always come across something you have never seen before. When examining any animal, it is sensible to remember the old saying that 'common conditions are seen most commonly', and not to jump to the conclusion that you are dealing with something strange and rare before you have ruled out the more frequently encountered ailments. Nevertheless, as a vet, I was always on the alert to expect the unexpected. Perhaps that would be a type of animal I had never treated before, an illness or condition I had never previously seen or perhaps a totally bizarre or unusual situation. Sometimes it could be a combination of all three.

I remember the time I was called to assist a llama in giving birth. I had treated alpacas but not llamas, so it was with a great deal of interest and perhaps a little trepidation that I drove up to the farm where a herd of around forty llamas were kept for breeding purposes. The female I had come to see had already been caught and put in a pen in the fields. I drove through the fields until I came upon a slightly nervous, clearly preoccupied llama looking haughtily down at me. The farmer put a head collar on her while I donned and soaped my arm-length gloves before putting my arm inside to examine her. I was told to take care as she might kick out; it is quite hard to be safe when you are standing directly behind an animal, but it is always sensible to be aware of the risks and to watch the body language of the animal, being ready to leap to one side if required. Another risk the vet faces when standing behind the animal with the complete length of their arm inside the animal trying to help the as yet unborn youngster is the risk that the animal may suddenly bend its legs and sink down or may suddenly fall or drop to the ground. Unless you can very quickly extract your arm, you risk a dislocated shoulder or even a broken bone. This was a great concern whenever I was asked to feel inside an animal, which was not very well mannered or, in other words, was likely to kick. The alternative could be to back the animal up to a stable door or perhaps place two straw bales one on top of the other close up to the hind end of the animal and reach over the door or the bales to examine inside the patient. This would help should she kick but would be very dangerous should she bend her legs and drop down.

Back to the llama, I could feel the cria's (baby llama) two front legs with the head coming in the correct presentation between the legs. This was a first-time mum, and she didn't have a lot of room for the cria to be delivered, but the baby was not oversized, so I judged she should be able to deliver normally with a little help from us. I attached a rope around the cria's head, placing it behind the ears to ensure it didn't slip off and attached one rope to each of the cria's front legs, and we began to pull in time with mum's straining. The cria started to move towards the outside world. It came through the pelvis, and then the two little hooves appeared in the world, with the little nose soon becoming visible between them. In a bovine calf, when the head has emerged, the neck and shoulders should follow quickly. This wasn't a calf though, it was a cria, and I was about to witness a big difference between a llama and a calf. I pulled some more; the legs were coming out, and the whole of the head was now delivered. I pulled again; the neck extended and extended and extended some more. I was beginning to worry; the neck was incredibly long, and the shoulders had not yet appeared. What had happened? I began to worry that the neck had dislocated, that I was doing some harm and was risking pulling it in two. I calmed myself and applied more lubricant to the baby. I had to keep pulling; it is dangerous for the cria to be left half in and half out. I pulled on the head again, more length of the neck came out; it was as though I were delivering a giraffe. At long last, the newborn's body appeared, then the hips and back legs, and in a joyous heave, a newborn cria was lying on the ground, grey and wet and beginning to shiver. I gave her a rub down then let mum take over. The little one was lying on the grass; she raised her head and made a little sound. Her neck was so long, like a periscope on top of her slim body and spindly legs. I knew she would look very different when she had dried out and was fluffy rather than wet and slimy and was standing up shakily walking around her mum looking for the 'milk bar'.

I had another opportunity to see her again sooner than I had bargained for. Late that day, the farmer rang to say the mum had retained her foetal membranes, could I go and check her out. It can be dangerous to mum not to get rid of the placenta, so I gave her medication to help it on its way. On this visit, the cria had transformed into a cute baby llama. It was so important mum didn't fall ill; she needed all her energy to look after her newly born baby.

Another first for me, but in a totally different way, was the time I was called, in a panic, to visit a much-loved family pony that lived in a steep field on one side of a dale but had somehow lost her footing and been found lying in the stream at the bottom of her field. I remember that it was approaching dusk as I put my hill-walking experience into action and found my way down the tussocks to where I could hear voices far below. The whole family was assembled to comfort Mistletoe, their Exmoor pony. They had managed to coax her out of the water, and she was standing dripping and looking very miserable. There was a small stable in the field where hay and straw were stored, so we all rubbed the little pony first with towels then with handfuls of hay to dry and warm her. Nothing seemed to be wrong apart from her feeling worse for wear after lying in the water for an unknown time. She started to graze and looked decidedly more cheerful. We moved her into the stable for the night and 'thatched' her; that is we put armfuls of hay on her back beneath her rug to form an insulating layer to keep her warm. Mistletoe's owners promised to check her over and remove the hay later that evening, by which time she should be nice and warm. They rang me the next day to say Mistletoe seemed back to her usual cheeky self and didn't seem to have suffered any lasting effects from her watery jaunt.

The little pony with hay under her rug

Some illnesses can be seen on a regular basis, but the particular circumstances surrounding them can cause one incident to stand out. I was very privileged to meet all kinds of people in my job, especially many 'Derbyshire characters' who represented a way of life now seldom seen. One elderly gentleman and his wife lived in a tumble-down stone farmhouse with few modern conveniences. The earth courtyard was edged by stone out-buildings; one of which had no roof tiles, only rafters silhouetted against the sky. The farmer owned some young stock and a few cows with calves at foot. When I visited one day, it was to attend a calving cow with a twisted uterus. The cows were all tied in the old barn or shippon as these barns were known, kept just as they had been by generations of farmers. The cows all had 'handlebar' horns sticking out either side of their head. In this case of the cow with the twisted womb, in order for her to deliver the calf, I would need to undo the twist in the uterus by 'rolling the cow'. First, I had to 'cast her' or lie her down on one side, then roll her onto her back with all four legs in the air and continue all the way over onto her other side and then stand her up. Just like a pet dog doing a trick, only this was a full-sized cow with large horns. Luckily for me, she was a small cow because the farmer was a small, elderly man and his wife remained firmly indoors, leaving me under no illusion that she would lend a hand. I knew she was watching us though, because I had spotted the curtain twitching when I first drove into the farmyard.

I had a look around and decided the best place to 'roll' the cow was on a piece of soft field just to the side of the barn. I threaded a rope over her back and underneath her belly in such a way that when you pull on the rope, it exerts pressure on the cow's back, and the animal should slowly sink to the ground. All was going well, very well, until the cow was lying upside down on her back in the mid-point of her roll.

"Push a bit harder; she's nearly there," I said to the farmer between gasps as I pushed as hard as I could. "What's holding her back?"

It was then that I realised the cow's very prominent upward-pointing pair of horns had sunk into the soft earth and were holding her firmly upside down on her back.

"It's her horns; she's stuck", I gasped to the farmer. "Can you pull her head up?"

That was when the farmer told me,

"I've gotta tek care. I canna do much lifting, I've a big 'ernia in me groin."

That is not what I wanted to hear.

At that very moment, the cow gave a huge wriggle and freed her horns from the earth. She completed her roll and sat up looking bemused. At the very same time, her waters broke, and a torrent of fluid burst forth from her back end. I breathed a huge sigh of relief, for this signified the torsion had undone, the rolling had been successful, and I could now deliver the calf.

CHAPTER NINETEEN
HAS ANYONE SEEN THE CAT?

Enjoying a sense of humour has always been an important part of my life. From fits of uncontrollable giggles when I was a child through practical jokes at someone else's expense to an ability to laugh at oneself is an important part of a vet's life. Sharing the good and the bad times is part of working with colleagues and clients alike and with both comes shared humour. Humour may help ease the tension or reduce worry when faced with an unfamiliar challenge; it may just be good-humoured wit and repartee between friends, it should be considered and not used when it could be hurtful. I think that the funny side of things often isn't appreciated until after the event.

It is true to say that I didn't find it funny when a wild suckler cow escaped from the crush when I was examining her and chased me across the yard, head lowered, her long horns pointing straight at me, she was bellowing and pawing the ground. I was really scared and ran across the yard looking for a means of escape. I spotted a large bale of silage in one corner, hauled myself up on top of it then scrambled up onto the oil tank where I felt safe. The cow smashed clean through the wooden gate at the yard entrance and trotted off up the road back to her field. I felt I'd had a narrow escape.

L ambing season is a very busy time for farmers and vets (and sheep!), and it can coincide with inclement weather. Here in the Peaks, many farmers lamb their flocks in later April and May to try to miss the severe weather, including deep snow that often occurs earlier in the year. Most sheep deliver their lambs with no problem at all and seeing a group of young lambs racing around the field enjoying life while their mums keep a concerned eye open for them whilst grazing the fresh green grass is a heart-lifting spectacle. Some sheep need a helping hand before they can deliver their lambs, and this is where I can help. One evening I returned to the surgery to meet a farmer client with a lovely large Texel ewe that had been looking uncomfortable for a while, as if she was about to go into labour, but things weren't progressing as expected, so she needed examining to see what was going on. Sarah, the farmer, reversed up to the lambing shed at the surgery, and I had a feel inside the ewe while Sarah restrained her for me in the back of their pickup. I could feel the ewe had not opened up inside even though she had been given plenty of time, already had lots of milk in her udder and was ready to give birth. The ultrasound scan performed on the ewe earlier in her pregnancy had shown she was carrying twins, and it was important we didn't wait too long, or we risked the lambs dying inside the ewe before they were born.

Our next step was to lift the ewe out of the pickup, walk her into the lambing shed then lift her up onto the operating table. Because I am not very tall (some may say I am really quite short), I am used to standing on stools to reach into cupboards or to finding that people have tidied my belongings up onto shelves I cannot reach. I had never before realised quite how high the table in our lambing shed was. It seemed particularly high when trying to lift up a very large, well-fleeced ewe carrying two lambs and all the associated foetal fluids. Sarah was quite diminutive too, we both counted to three then together we lifted the ewe, we couldn't see over the top of her, her woolly fleece was completely obscuring my vision, we staggered towards the table, but were a little low, and as we tilted the ewe to place her on the table, the table began to tip too. Sometimes, when things aren't going quite according to plan, a sort of anxiety makes me giggle, and that happened now. Not just to me but to Sarah too, we were both laughing and staggering around under the weight of the monster sheep, and of course, the more we laughed, the weaker we became. I took some deep breaths, and with a final heave, the ewe was lying on her side on the table where I made her secure before starting to prepare her for surgery. Because her abdomen was so distended by her pregnancy, I couldn't even see the area I was going to be operating on. So, I performed the complete caesarean section standing on a stool. It must have worked well as two lovely live twins were the happy result and a ewe that felt a great deal more comfortable than beforehand. After the operation, Sarah and I managed to lift the ewe down from the table and up into the back of the pickup with no problem at all due to her being two lambs and a large volume of fluid lighter than before her operation.

Home visits to examine pets can be very convenient and possibly less stressful for the pet and the owner than visiting the surgery, but at times the situation can present unusual problems for the vet. Cats are masters at concealing themselves and disappearing in a room where you are sure there is absolutely nowhere for your favourite moggy to hide. When requested to visit a poorly cat called Tiger, I knew I should have asked his owner to shut the door to the kitchen before she fed Tiger his breakfast, then we would have him captive, but somehow the door was open just a crack, and he disappeared and is now nowhere to be found.

"He knew you were coming, you know, I'm sure he did, and he's hidden. I've looked everywhere in the house, searched every room, but I can't find him," the owner declared.

Once I had ascertained all windows were closed, and the aptly named Tiger couldn't have escaped into the garden, I started a systematic search. I was experienced in knowing where a clever cat might conceal itself.

Top of the list was under the bed. This was a small cottage having only one bedroom, a small blessing for the vet at least. The bed was an old wooden double bed with a hand-crocheted bedspread reaching to the floor on all sides. With a certain amount of trepidation, I got down on my hands and knees on the floor and slowly raised the crocheted cover; I didn't want an angry or frightened Tiger taking a swipe at my head with his front claws.

There he was, not waiting to pounce at all but lying on the carpet right bang in the centre of the area of the bed, watching with disdain. This was a bit of a conundrum. We tried enticing him from his safe spot, where he was out of reach of owners and vets, by talking sweetly to him and offering his favourite food but to no avail. So, under the bed, I squeezed and squirmed until I managed to nudge Tiger out of his hiding place and into the arms of his owner. At last, the main purpose of the visit could begin.

The cat hiding from the vet

CHAPTER TWENTY

TRAVELS WITH A TORTOISE

Over the years, I have been privileged to treat many different kinds of animals. As well as dogs, cats, horses and farm animals (which is quite a long list in itself), there are budgies, pet chickens, injured wildlife, guinea pigs, hamsters, rabbits, snakes, bearded dragons, goldfish and the tarantula that I had to ask my colleague to come in and examine for me.

I had the good fortune of visiting the prize-winning birds belonging to pigeon fanciers and being able to look around the lofts where their pigeons were kept. Pigeon racing is a popular sport in Derbyshire a sport with which I was not familiar, I enjoyed these visits and the chance to learn from people who had kept and raced pigeons for many years and whose parents frequently had done the same before them. There is something very soothing about seeing well-cared-for pigeons cooing and strutting around in their coops, and of hearing tales from their enthusiastic, knowledgeable owners of races won and lost. I learnt so much about the individual birds and their husbandry. As a vet, I had knowledge of diseases and parasites that pigeons suffer from, but these are crucially bound up with how the pigeons are kept and their environment. It can sometimes be useful to take a diagnostic sample from a pigeon, then later to examine the sample under the microscope back at the surgery or to send it to a specialist laboratory. Faeces samples in cases of diarrhoea can be very revealing as to the most likely cause of the problem. If a pigeon falls ill and does not recover, a post-mortem examination can be performed to ascertain the cause of death. If I need to investigate a case in this way, I may ask the owner for samples to be taken from several birds to aid in making a diagnosis. One day when I arrived early at work, I found a large brown envelope pushed through the letterbox with my name on it. I was excited. What could this be? I certainly was not expecting what I found. Written on the back flap of the envelope in small, neat writing were the words 'Pigeon Snot'. One of my pigeon fancier clients had helpfully sent a diagnostic sample.

One of the highlights of the Bakewell year for animal lovers is the annual carnival week Pet Show, a very popular event generously supported by the local pet shop, which doesn't sell pets but sells everything associated with our four-legged friends. I was asked to judge the pet show several times, and it really kept me on my toes. I felt it was an honour to be asked to judge and recognised how carefully I must tread to avoid hurting anyone's feelings while at the same time making sure the pets that were given prizes were those who deserved them. With several classes and upwards of twenty-five pets in a class, it is only too easy to give one pet more than one rosette while another equally cute and well-behaved pooch may go home empty-pawed.

I found some of the classes especially hard to judge, one such was the 'best in show' where the pets placed first in each class were judged against each other. The individual classes were 'cutest dog', 'dog with the waggiest tail', 'best-kept rabbit' and 'most unusual pet'. Judging a stick insect, a cute small furry dog, a loving rescue dog, and a large white rabbit against each other has its challenges.

The class I had to think about most carefully before making my award was 'The pet that looks most like its owner'. Some owners wore elaborate fancy dress to mimic their Yorkshire Terrier for example, and others had perhaps grown to resemble their dog over the years, sometimes in stature or maybe in facial expression. I do remember my choice that day being very hairy, possibly a little rotund but very well mannered.

One year I became well acquainted with a much-travelled tortoise called Horace. I describe him as much-travelled because his lovely elderly owner didn't drive, so every Monday, market day in Bakewell; she would put Horace in a zip-up shopping bag and bring him into town on the bus. Horace hadn't been very well when he came out of hibernation and now required regular weighing to determine if his health was improving. At the surgery, he would be bathed, his mouth cleaned and treated for infection, then he would be fed by stomach tube. These procedures were repeated a few times until he started to eat on his own again. I remember with delight the day his owner rang me to describe how Horace had walked into her garden, opened his jaws very wide and polished off a bright yellow dandelion flower in one mouthful. I missed Horace's visits to the surgery, but I was so pleased he had returned to full health.

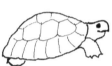

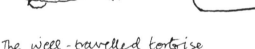

The well-travelled tortoise

Some weeks later, I visited Horace at home to check on his progress. His sleeping box was in an old-fashioned potting shed surrounded by stacks of large terracotta flowerpots. He could wander out of the shed at will through a small hole cut into the bottom of the wooden door and then had the 'run' of the garden and all the goodies growing in the border. It was like a pick your own salad and sweet bar combined. We made sure he was in good health before he hibernated that autumn, so he had no problems when he awoke the following spring.

I 've always had a soft spot for guinea pigs, but the little lady guinea pig 'Millie' looked very different from usual when she came to the surgery one day. Her owner said she was still eating her food in her usual quantities, but she couldn't understand why Millie's tummy was so very large. She confirmed Millie had not been with a male guinea pig, so there was no risk of her being pregnant. I had to confess I hadn't seen a guinea pig with such a huge abdomen before, so I suggested I should perform an ultrasound examination to see what was going on. We clipped Millie's tummy and put some lubricant on it before gently putting the ultrasound probe against her skin. I soon diagnosed her problem; she had a massive ovarian cyst which would need surgically removing. This proved to be a delicate but rewarding operation. After the operation, I measured the cyst to be six inches (fifteen centimetres) in diameter. Poor little Millie was only a bit longer than that herself. She made a quick and uneventful recovery and was soon running around squeaking as normal.

Chapter Twenty-One
Oh Dear!

A significant part of a vet's day is spent dealing with routine procedures which become very familiar over time. Some can become a little too familiar, especially when they involve something unpleasant.

All dogs have anal sacs or anal glands as they are often called; these are small structures containing a strong malodorous substance that is discharged by the dog when it defecates, leaving a scent marker for other dogs to sniff and interpret. In this natural event, neither the dogs nor their owners are aware of the existence of these small glands. The structures are sometimes eloquently described as being 'the size of seedless grapes', a description that seems quite inappropriate for something so smelly. The dog can't feel the glands and is totally unaware of their existence until something goes wrong.

The glands can become blocked, meaning they can no longer empty when your pooch goes to the toilet. The anal glands become enlarged, impacted and irritant for the poor dog. Now, as you can imagine, a dog does not have the ability to scratch its bottom with its paw or to say to its owner that it has a sore bottom, so a situation arises when the poor dog can't relieve the pain caused by the blocked glands. You may become aware of your dog licking its backside or desperately trying to lick the area, but much more likely, you will notice your beloved hound scooting across your very best light beige carpet with a peculiar 'marching' action of the hind legs and a very determined look on their face.

It is time to ring the vets and let someone else have the pleasure of examining the offending area.

Most anal gland irritations clear up very quickly after the anal glands are manually expressed or 'emptied' by the vet. Performing this procedure is usually painless for the dog, the owner and the vet, but sometimes it can prove a little more problematic than others. The poor dog has a sore backside and may be nervous about what is going to happen when approached by a glove-wearing vet holding wads of cotton wool.

One day a small, very hairy, very cute much-loved terrier came to see me during consultations. He had been spotted scooting on his bottom, and his smart, well-dressed owner had brought him down as soon as she was free. Everything was going according to plan; I had made a fuss of Bubbles (for that was the little dog's name), he always greeted me like a long-lost friend, and I was very fond of him. An examination revealed discomfort caused by enlarged anal sacs, which I prepared to empty. The little dog was standing on the examination table with the owner expertly holding his front end whilst whispering gently in his ear. I held his tail up in the air with one hand and deftly squeezed the anal sacs using my gloved other hand. Once I applied pressure, the foul-smelling contents shot out explosively in a brown, liquid stream, but alas, they missed the wad of clean cotton wool I was holding in which to catch the offensive fluid. At first, I wasn't sure what had happened, the cotton wool was empty, but I was certain I had seen the contents of the glands being expelled in a horrible jet of fluid. Then reality dawned, there was a dark brown streak dribbling down the front of a very expensive beige leather handbag placed out of the way on the consulting room floor.

Another anal sac consultation that left an unpleasant smell lingering concerned a bright and cheery Westie called Masie, a dog with lots of character who was always in a good mood. I had emptied her anal sacs on numerous previous occasions without a problem; I presumed this time would be the same. After initially squeezing the glands, I wasn't satisfied they were completely empty and decided they needed further examination. I bent down to better see the area in question and deduce what was stopping the glands from expelling all their contents. I felt around the area. It was as I had thought, the sac was still full, but at least Masie was keeping still and behaving like a very good girl. Oh dear, I had spoken too soon; she must have had enough. As I gently felt her anal sacs, she uttered a little bark and bounced forward on the table; at the same time, her anal sac emptied itself, and the horrible contents shot straight out into my hair!

Even after several washes, I could smell the indescribable fishy odour clinging to me, following me around for the rest of the day.

One of my favourite patients was a very handsome cat called Tabitha. She was not as young as she used to be and was drinking a lot more water than usual. I had run some tests and discussed an ongoing treatment plan with Tabitha's lovely owner. When Tabitha refused her food one day, I was asked if I would go and visit her at home. When I arrived at the smart and spacious bungalow, I was shown into the sitting room and invited to sit down on one of the pale cream leather armchairs. Tabitha was sitting in the bay window, watching the world go by. She let me pick her up and examine her, purring all the time. When I put her back down, she came over to my chair and jumped up onto my lap, where she curled up contentedly. Her owner said it was fine for her to sit on the chairs; she was allowed to go wherever she liked in the house. I had been offered a coffee, and as I sat sipping it and discussing Tabitha's progress, I slowly became aware of a warm feeling spreading out from my lap, along my legs. My heart missed a beat, and I feel sure I blanched. I hadn't felt I needed the toilet; surely I hadn't had an accident?

I didn't know what to do. Should I stand up and hope

it was just the warm feeling due to Tabitha lying curled up on my knees?

Then I realised what had happened. Tabitha had been unable to control herself and had urinated on my lap. Recently she had been drinking substantially more than normal, and that meant she would be weeing a lot more too.

I took a deep breath. Gingerly I picked Tabitha up and stood up. I hardly dared turn to look at the cream leather armchair; what if it had a big wet mark on it?

Luckily, there was no mark on the chair. Luckily, my trousers were a dark colour, and the wetness wasn't obvious. I picked up my visit bag and held it in front of my thighs as I walked from the house. As I placed the bag in the boot of my car, I took out a large clean polythene bag and placed it on my car seat. I said my goodbyes and drove back to my house for a shower and a much-needed change of clothes.

CHAPTER TWENTY-TWO
HELP!

The car journey from surgery to or from a farm provides useful time to collect one's thoughts about the call you are about to attend. It provides space to formulate a structured plan based on the knowledge you have of the premises, type of stock, the handling facilities, help and experience available and many other variables. Each situation needs to be assessed at the time. You may know only scant details of what you are going to see and must keep an open mind and be aware of not making assumptions before you arrive. I often knew the owners, what stock they had, plus a good knowledge of the premises beforehand, but every visit brings new challenges.

One day I found myself visiting a secluded farm to examine some coughing calves. Pneumonia in calves housed together in a group is common; sick calves need treating before they deteriorate and the situation as a whole needs to be assessed to prevent spread to the rest of the stock. On the journey to the farm, I had been going over in my mind the likely causes of the disease and ways to prevent and minimise the problem.

I drove down the drive and drew up in front of the house. I knew the farmer was likely to be round the back in the cattle shed and that the house may be empty. I put on my wellingtons, gathered my stethoscope, thermometer and other equipment and started to walk across the grass. It was then that I became aware of the sound of crowing and a blur of gold and red flashed in front of my eyes.

I didn't see the cockerel until he rushed at me; he leapt up to my waist height with the sharp, curved fighting spurs on the back of his legs pointing straight at me.

I tried to fend him off with the box I was holding while at the same time trying to run backwards, but again, and again he lunged at me with his talons ready to draw blood. I was calling for help, stumbling backwards as best I could at the same time as watching the bird attack me from in front. I was frightened. After what seemed like a long, long time, the farmer appeared round the corner of the barn. He chased away the angry bird and rescued me.

I was shaken and had to compose myself as I walked towards the calves to begin the real task of the afternoon.

A nother scary situation occurred late one afternoon when the day was drawing in, and darkness had already enveloped the hills. I was called to a large, isolated stone house set high on the moorland where the north wind whistled with nothing to break its howling journey. I had visited the house before and nicknamed it 'Wuthering Heights' due to its bleak appearance and rather taciturn incumbent. The house was tall and square and stood at the end of a dead straight driveway approached from a single-track lane that strode across the moorland and was usually blocked by snow at least once each winter.

The scary house in a gale

I had been called to the farm to castrate some of the older calves. As I drove up the drive, the rain started to lash down to complement the gale blowing from the north. Several windows in the house seemed open or perhaps had no glass in them, and the faded curtains were blowing outwards like sails. I parked and, as quickly as possible layered myself in waterproofs. Then equipped with my torch, I entered the dark, tumbledown barn in order to look for the farmer and let him know I had arrived. I was desperately hoping that there would be somewhere reasonably secure to restrain the calves while I castrated them. These young cattle were nearly old enough to be interested in mating the female cattle they shared their pasture with and needed 'seeing too' as soon as possible. As I walked through the gloom of the barn, I found myself imagining ghostly figures looming out of the darkness, lurking in the corners beyond the beam of my head torch.

Eventually, I found the farmer waiting alongside the calves, which were in a small enclosure in the corner of the barn. The farmer had borrowed a 'crush' or mobile cage in which to secure each animal while it was being examined and castrated. Luckily the handling facilities were fit for purpose, not on this occasion held together by baler twine, so the job was soon completed, and I made my way back out through the pouring rain to the car.

I wasn't sorry to be driving away; this place gave me the shivers. The rain was lashing sideways in the beam of the headlights, the surrounding moor as black as night. At the bottom of the drive are two high, square stone gateposts leading onto the narrow lane. I turned onto the lane and immediately found my path was blocked. I couldn't go any further. I didn't really know if I was dreaming or if my mind had been influenced by the weather and the scary surroundings. But lying right across my path, blocking the whole width of the lane, was a dead cow.

I got out into the downpour and checked that the unfortunate beast definitely had no life left in it. I was struggling to think how it could have got there in the half an hour since I had previously passed that way. There were no marks on it, no marks on the road or grass verge. However, there was no room for me to drive past with it lying there. I had no phone reception up here on the moor; I certainly didn't fancy retracing my steps to 'Wuthering Heights'. What should I do?

I noticed the cow had never been disbudded as a calf and now sported long curved horns from the top of her head. Grabbing those, I managed with great difficulty to swivel her one way then the other until I saw I was gradually moving her to one side of the road giving sufficient room for me to inch past in the car.

When eventually I arrived back at the surgery, I was able to phone the farmer and arrange to have the beast removed. I secretly hoped I didn't have to visit that farm again in a hurry.

CHAPTER TWENTY-THREE

NETTLE RASH

"Ah, that's where the tarts come from" was a frequent reply when I told people where I lived. The tarts being referred to here are known as Bakewell tarts, the iced almond sponge in a pastry case with a cherry on top. These delicacies are not the ones for which the local market town of Bakewell is renowned. The famous pastries are, in fact, Bakewell puddings, which originated due to a chef's mistake when the flour was inadvertently left out of the recipe. The Bakewell pudding is a sweet, firm almond custard sitting on raspberry jam in a puff pastry case. In my opinion best eaten warm with custard.

I soon came to know of other local delicacies such as the warm pork pies straight from the butcher or the delicacies which could be foraged from the hedgerows between calls when time allowed. One farm I visited was on an ancient site reached through lanes bordered mostly by drystone walls, but some were overhung by hedges, less usual in this part of the country. The farmer had rung with the message that he'd found a 'cow calving down near the stream'. This could be an emergency and needed seeing as soon as possible. The cow was having difficulty calving and may need assistance; I wondered if the message meant the cow was down on her side or was she in the field down near to the stream, could she be about to wander into the stream and get herself stuck? Many thoughts raced through my head as I jumped in the car and drove through the lanes making sure I arrived at the farm as soon as possible. It was a lovely autumn morning with the dew still heavy on the grass when the farmer and I walked down through the lush fields towards the stream. I was wearing over trousers and my waterproof smock and carrying everything I might need for the task in hand: lubricant, calving ropes, calving jack in case some extra pull was needed, local anaesthetic in case she should need an epidural to stop her straining and anything else I could think of which would fit into my carrier. The farmer carried a bucket of warm water and soap. When we reached the cow, she was lying flat out on her side, unable to rise, she was indeed quite near the stream, but that was the least of her (and my) worries. Beside her was a little calf, still wet and glistening as the mother hadn't been able to lick it dry. I took in all of these details with the first glance. I also saw that behind the cow was her large, pink, fleshy, freshly prolapsed womb. This uterus had inverted or turned itself inside out and been pushed outside the body by the cow straining following the birth of the calf. This huge mound of flesh (imagine the size of a full to bursting old fashioned hessian sack) needed replacing as soon as possible to stop it from becoming damaged and bleeding and to stop the cow from going into shock and possibly dying.

As if this wasn't enough to contend with, I also noticed something else which was not a welcome sight – the cow was lying right bang in the middle of the largest, most mature patch of nettles I had ever seen. I knew that in order to replace the prolapsed uterus back inside the cow, I would have to kneel down behind the cow with her inverted uterus on my lap, and after thoroughly cleaning it, I would have to gently but forcibly push it back in. When, after a lot of effort, it was back in place inside the cow, I would have to lie down at full stretch to reach inside her to make sure the uterus was completely back to its normal position.

First, I knelt down behind the recumbent cow and gave her an injection to stop her straining and trying to push out more of her insides; then with the soap and water, I washed the red raw prolapsed mass, being careful not to tear it and enhance the cow's chances of going into shock which could easily be fatal. I gently removed any afterbirth still stuck to the uterus. Then I started to push the heavy squashy mass back into its rightful place inside the cow. Starting nearest to the cow and holding the uterus on my knees, I pushed and pushed and pushed again. I tried to ignore my legs screaming with pins and needles and my arms and face being stung by the jungle of nettles which almost obscured me. At last, the end was in sight and with one last push, all was back inside the cow.

Next, I lay down behind her to reach as far into the uterus as possible to ensure it was totally back in place. I knew that if even the tiniest portion was inverted, one push by the cow probably when I had just got to bed, and the whole lot would be out again, bursting through the stitches I was just about to insert.

After all was back in its rightful place, the farmer and I positioned the cow so she was lying in a more upright position where she could have a long drink of water and steady herself; and most importantly, relieve herself by belching out the gas which becomes trapped in a cow's stomach when lying flat out on their side.

I was pleased with the job done, more than can be said for my appearance. I was boiling hot under my full-length waterproof gown, which was now wet and sticky with blood and fluid from the newly calved cow. My skin was red and stinging from a million nettles. I must have looked a fright. I certainly felt one. Several buckets of clean water, soap and a hose pipe helped.

So did the cup of tea and homemade cake back at the farmhouse.

But best of all, on the way back up the hedge-lined farm drive, I noticed brambles laden with ripe, glistening, mouth-wateringly delicious blackberries.

I must stop and pick some. I deserve some! What container have I got with me to collect them in? Travelling around in a car kitted out for many veterinary eventualities, you can almost always find something to help even a non-veterinary situation. This time, my eye alighted on the box of new arm length plastic rectal gloves used for pregnancy diagnosis in cows, for lambings, and of course for filling with juicy blackberries. I chuckled when I put my blackberries straight from the hedgerow into the top of the glove, and they tumbled down the sleeve to fill each of the fingers and the thumb and then the whole hand. To stop the filled glove rolling around the floor of the car as I drove along the winding lanes, I popped it into my Wellington boot; a good place too for storing a bottle should you happen to stop at a corner shop on your way home in the evening.

CHAPTER
TWENTY-FOUR
MIRACLES DO HAPPEN

O ne of the farms I visited regularly was down a
very long rough stone track which wound
through the fields for over a mile. This farm
had a large flock of sheep and lots of suckler cows which
roamed over a large acreage; all the stock here had wild
temperaments and didn't take kindly to being handled by
a vet. The farming family also owned competition horses,
and some horses were kept at livery. Visits during the
calving season, lambing season and eventing season could
be frequent.

One late afternoon I was called out to see a newly born
calf that had 'something hanging from its navel'. This is an
alarming description for a vet to hear; sometimes, a calf
can be born with a weakness in the body wall around the
navel, and when the mother cow licks her calf after birth,
the navel can split, and part of the guts literally fall out like
a tangled red mass onto the floor of the calving pen. At
best, the pen will be thickly bedded with clean straw,

however far too often the floor will be muddy, or the guts will just happen to land right in the middle of a soft, warm cowpat. I had all these thoughts going through my mind as I sped down the dirt track, skidding around corners and leaving the track to drive on the dry grass of the adjoining field when the track became extra rocky.

The calf born approximately one hour earlier was lying on a dirt floor. Eva, the farmer's wife, had removed the mother cow up to the other end of the large barn so she would not inadvertently cause more damage to the calf or become over-protective when we were helping her calf.

At first glance, my worst fears were confirmed. A large mass of deep red coloured intestines had prolapsed through the umbilicus and were lying, still attached to the rest of the guts inside the calf, in the muck and dirt on the floor of the shed. Eva had already prepared some buckets of warm, clean water, we spread some straw on the ground, and with Eva holding the calf on its back, I tried to wash the guts. Small bits of dirt were stuck to every bit of the prolapsed intestine. The calf resented being held on its back, so I gave it a small dose of sedative, which enabled us to hold it up as if it was standing on its four legs while I washed the guts protruding from the middle of its tummy in a bucket of water placed between the four legs of the calf. After laying the calf back down and anaesthetising the area, with great difficulty, I was able to replace the many feet of guts back inside the calf where they belonged. Eva and I gave the calf some liquid food by stomach tube then let its mum return to her calf's side so she could mother it. If luck was on our side, the calf might soon want to suck some of the mother's milk.

The chances of the calf recovering without sustaining an internal infection were very small, and it was with great trepidation a few days later that I made the phone call.

"Eva, it's Lorna, how's that calf?

"Oh, she's fine, she was up and sucking her mum later in the evening, and now she's back outside racing around like nothing's ever been wrong."

That news made me feel on top of the world. The calf had survived against the odds; luck had been shining on us that evening.

Chapter Twenty-Five

Childhood Memories

When we were children, my sister and I were mad about ponies. For many years we didn't have a real pony but spent countless hours playing on our pretend ponies, nowadays we might call them virtual ponies, which we rode around the garden and took to pretend gymkhanas. We jumped over obstacles made from fallen branches and made rosettes from paper then coloured them, always red to show we had won first prize. We progressed to having weekly riding lessons at a local riding school on real ponies, and then we rode a pony belonging to a friend of a friend. We had many hours of fun and laughter. Then one magical day, we had ponies of our own. We rented a field several miles from our house and cycled there and back each day with the ponies' saddles on the handlebars of our bikes.

As well as cycling for miles, we rode the ponies for miles every day. I remember galloping along narrow overgrown paths through bluebell woods, almost out of control, nearly colliding with tree trunks but always laughing and having a great time. We trekked long distances to local shows where we took part in 'pony, kit and tack' classes or 'bending' races. We picnicked in fields golden with buttercups. I loved it all.

On the day before I was due to go to university to begin my veterinary studies, my pony became ill with severe colic (abdominal pain). He was in tremendous pain, was sweating and had stomach contents refluxing down his nose. I now know a lot about this serious condition called 'Grass Sickness', but I wasn't so well informed then. Looking back, I can empathise with what the vet was going through as he tried to treat my pony and then had to break the news to me that the pony would not get better and to arrange for him to be euthanised before he suffered further pain. They were very sad days. I have since experienced first-hand the emotions of desperately upset owners, and I often remember back to that last night before I left home to study in a city many miles away, where at first, I knew no one. It was with a heavy heart and red, puffy eyes that I began my first term studying veterinary surgery at university.

CHAPTER TWENTY-SIX
JOURNEY TO THE CENTRE OF THE EARTH

Horses come in all shapes and sizes, I have treated shire horses, and I have treated miniature Shetlands and most sizes in between. There is an old saying, 'No foot, no 'oss', meaning a lame horse is no good for work or pleasure. Most horses are used to having their hooves cleaned and checked for stones or for cuts every time they are ridden. Unfortunately, sharp pieces of grit or an old rusty nail may still manage to penetrate the soft tissues and lead to pus in the foot, an intensely painful condition for the horse. When there is no damage to vital structures like tendons or joints, infection can often be successfully treated by establishing and maintaining drainage. I was frequently requested to attend to the feet of a lovely little donkey who was afflicted with recurring infections due to suffering from misshapen feet. Fortunately, she was rescued by a very caring owner, but it took many visits before Genevieve grew to trust me, and I was able to pare all four of her dainty little hooves without needing to quieten her down with a sedative injection beforehand.

P onies and horses are all too often afflicted by coughs. Coughs have many causes; among the most common are allergic conditions and viral infections, often with bacterial complications. Whatever the cause, a cough is potentially serious. If it is infectious, there's the risk of spread to other horses, and a coughing horse should not be exercised, which is not ideal if it is the middle of the summer and you have entered a horse show.

Some coughs last for only a short time, and with the appropriate treatment and management, the patient soon recovers. In others, the cough never goes away completely, but the owner learns how to manage the condition and look after the horse in such a way that the cough is minimal.

In order to find out exactly what is causing a horse to cough, I would frequently carry out a further diagnostic test using a fibre optic endoscope. A veterinary endoscope is a marvellous diagnostic tool that comes in various lengths (from a few centimetres to a few metres) and enables the user to see inside places they would not normally be able to see inside.

If a horse had excessively noisy breathing when it cantered or galloped or when I wanted to find out the underlying reason why a horse was coughing, or if a horse had a thick, smelly discharge from its nose, I would use an endoscope to visually examine up the horse's nose and down the trachea or windpipe to find the underlying cause. Horses sometimes need to be injected with a sedative before this procedure is carried out, but this is not always the case; many tolerate it very well without sedation. An endoscope is essentially a tiny camera and light at the end of a long flexible tube. There are additional channels in the tube to allow you to inject fluids or siphon fluids away or allow you to use forceps to take biopsies down the tube or to retrieve foreign bodies. (e.g., from the windpipe if something like a seed has been inhaled or from a dog's stomach if it has swallowed something small).

Introducing an endoscope up a horse's nose and being able to see the anatomy all the way up the long nasal passage and into the throat, to visualise in full Technicolor the very back of the mouth where the vocal cords are moving is quite remarkable. You can see the blood vessels as they run under the surface; you are aware of particles of food or flecks of pus in places you don't want to find them. If you want to take a diagnostic sample from the lungs, you continue your journey through the throat and down the windpipe. It is like being on a Jules Verne Journey to the Centre of the Earth. You forget you are standing in a cold stable yard with one eye pressed to the end of a long tube and your other hand partially inserted into the horse's nostril holding the tube in place. You are transported to another world of reds and browns with curves and bulges, where surfaces gleam and glisten, and bubbles appear as you continue along the tunnel-like onward journey. You can move the far end of the endoscope in multiple directions so you can examine the affected area in detail. You can gaze at the walls of the passage, turn corners to enter large chambers or sinuses in the head, you can check the relative positions of the structures to each other, or you can look for spots of blood or areas of damage.

When you have explored the whole area and taken any samples you need, you gently remove the endoscope from the nostril, and suddenly you are back in the real world once more. You are still standing in the yard with a horse in front of you; you have samples to label and forms to write. But in your imagination, you've been to the centre of the earth along fantastic magical pathways, witnessed intricate science in motion – what an experience.

I frequently treated pets with allergies, and ponies were well represented amongst this number. Sweet itch is a horrible condition for a pony to suffer. It is an allergic reaction to being bitten by a certain type of midge, which makes the pony incredibly itchy along its mane and at the top of the tail. The poor pony rubs and rubs these areas until they are raw.

It must be incredibly uncomfortable, and removing the pony from the area preferred by the midges is one of the best management options. Another thing that I found helped the afflicted pony was for the owner to purchase a specially designed horse rug made from a specific material that prevented the midges from biting through it. The rug fits over the horse's head and ears and encloses as much of the body as possible, so the end result is that the horse ends up looking like an old-fashioned jousting horse.

I remember visiting a donkey who suffered from sweet itch; her owner and I duly measured the donkey for one of these bespoke rugs and sent off for one. When it arrived, I had to laugh. The ears on the hood part of the rug were about twice as long as the donkey's ears! This was not at all important to the donkey as she didn't have a mirror, and I hope she didn't mind me laughing at her. Thankfully the rug was very effective, and this lovely donkey no longer itched and rubbed herself raw and could spend her days peacefully grazing.

CHAPTER TWENTY-SEVEN

KIDS

One day I got a call to go and visit lovely Doris, who kept goats. She was very knowledgeable, having shown and bred goats for many years. She had recently branched out into cheese making, and her cheeses won many awards at the same agricultural shows where her goats won many rosettes. Most of her goats were the brown and white Toggenburg breed, while some were Anglo Nubians, famous for their haughty Roman nose. Over the years, I had come to know Doris and her goats very well, having been called to examine them and keep them healthy. Whenever they were off their food or were lame or needed a blood sample taken for routine health checks, I would go and visit. The goats lived outside in the fields in summer or in cosy pens bedded with clean straw if they needed special care or when the weather was cold and wet or snowy. I love most things about goats. I love their personality, their charm and the cuteness of the kids. There is one thing that I do not like about goats though, and that is the strong musky, sweetish smell given off by the billy goats. Doris only had one billy, but that was enough. I always knew when he was near by the strong and all-enveloping odour which hung in the still air; it clung to my clothes, lingered on my gloves and invaded my senses. I would dress in protective clothing, put a scarf on my head and always wear gloves. I would take his blood sample as swiftly as I could and then hose myself down. I could never remove the smell entirely. It didn't leave me until I had a complete change of clothes and a shower at home!

But on this spring day, I was going to be fine, smell-wise. I was going to visit one of the female goats who was struggling to give birth, or kid. Goats usually kid on their own and have one or maybe two kids; it is only very occasionally that they need a helping hand. Perhaps both kids are trying to come out at once with a head and leg belonging to one twin trying to exit at the same time as a leg from another twin. Perhaps there is a backside presented instead of a head, or sometimes there is not enough room for a kid however small to be born the natural way. When I arrived, Doris greeted me and showed me to the pen where Maisie the Toggenburg mum was standing with tail raised, looking a little 'quaint' as they say in Derbyshire, meaning 'not quite right'. She knew something was not progressing as it should. I donned my waterproof gown and arm length disposable gloves, lubricated my arm and felt inside.

"Maisie is glad it's you; you've small arms," said Doris.

Maisie was being very patient, letting me examine her

while she stood still. I soon determined her problem. She had been wanting to kid for a few hours but was not dilating. We could not leave her very much longer, or her kids would not live. There was only one thing to do.

"They won't come out this way Doris, I'll have to operate. She needs a caesarean"

Doris sprang into action. We soon had a straw bale for a table, two buckets of clean, warm water, more clean straw under Maisie, who was standing up tied by her halter to the wooden railing. I collected my sterile instrument pack from the car, the medications I would need, a razor and special soap for sterilising the area on her side once I had shaved it down to the soft skin beneath the brown hair. Maisie would remain standing throughout. The area was numbed with local anaesthetic so Maisie would feel nothing as I cut through the skin and then the muscle layers and felt right inside her abdomen to the uterus. I could feel the hind leg of a kid as it lay inside the uterus. I grasped it and gently pulled it to the hole I had made. The leg felt quite small, even for a baby goat kid. I cut into the uterus and pulled the kid out through the hole I'd made, then handed it to Doris, who laid it in the straw and checked it was breathing and all was OK. I put my hand back into the uterus where I felt another kid – a twin, how lovely. This one was alive too. Mother was not too worried about what I was doing, so the kids were put in the straw near her head, and she started to lick them while I put my hand back to check the uterus prior to suturing it closed. Imagine my surprise when I felt another kid. No wonder the leg had been small; there were triplets.

The third one was soon safely delivered, and I began to close the wound, first the uterus, then the muscle layers and finally the skin.

What a lovely sight I saw when I had cleaned up and was ready to go: mother Masie with three healthy kids already standing and wagging their little tails and trying to suck their first milk meal.

"A lovely job," said Doris. "Now we've got to think of three names. I'd like to call one of them Lorna – would you mind?"

I was delighted and felt very privileged, and that is how there is a goat near Bakewell that answers to the name of Lorna.

CHAPTER TWENTY-EIGHT

WHAT WILL TODAY BRING?

When I went into work each morning, I would never be sure what surprises the day would hold. I would already know from our rota if I was going to be consulting in the surgery, working my way through the day's operating list or whether I had farm or horse visits booked. But I never knew what situation I might encounter on my travels or what emergency might be rushed into the practice, or what interesting cases would come into the consulting room.

I loved working with many different animals, but I also loved getting to meet and know their owners. Interacting with people is a large part of a vet's life in a veterinary practice, and to me this was a very special part of my work. I loved meeting the different Derbyshire characters and having the opportunity to talk to so many interesting people.

A lot of the daily tasks performed are routine, but always varied. I clipped the claws of pets as wide-ranging as hamsters, Guinea pigs, tiny Chihuahua dogs, all sorts and colours of Spaniels, Saint Bernards weighing 80Kg (12 stone 6lb) and Irish Wolfhounds standing over 76cm tall (2 foot 6 inches). I examined lumps on budgerigars, became acquainted with parrots who were excessively plucking out their feathers, I saw lame dogs of various shapes and sizes, cats with fleas, dogs and cats with sore ears, friendly dogs with bad teeth, unfriendly snarling dogs with bad teeth, I emptied foul-smelling anal glands, treated dogs who had diarrhoea, advised about vomiting dogs and cats, cats who were losing weight, rabbits with flystrike and the list goes on. Being a vet is never boring. Even the more routine vaccinations are interesting, frequently being the first opportunity to meet a delightful, cuddly new puppy or kitten.

A vet is always working to a timetable. Morning consultations must be completed before operations can begin. Operations need to be finished in time for evening consultations. Messages must be dealt with, owners contacted, laboratory results reported, unusual or difficult cases discussed with colleagues, x-rays interpreted, meetings set up and attended. When I was lucky, I would have some 'me' time to eat lunch.

Many of the surgical operations booked in would be routine in nature. Most days, there would be one or more cats or dogs to neuter. Frequently I would examine a pet during consults and, because of the serious nature of the illness, would know that we would have to operate on it that day, so the pet would be admitted and spend the day with us, or longer if needed. Perhaps a pet would have suffered an accident, maybe a skin wound from getting caught on barbed wire, or perhaps a dog that had stood on a shard of glass and was bleeding all over the carpets as it walked around the house or sadly those pets who had been involved in a road traffic accident and had been rushed in as an emergency.

A bitch may be having trouble whelping and would need immediate attention. If, after examination and medication, pups were not able to be born naturally, then a caesarean section would be required. The whole veterinary team loved a caesarean section, and this sort of operation is very much a team effort. My nurses would not only prepare the bitch for surgery and monitor her anaesthetic throughout the procedure, but they would take hold of the puppies as I brought them out through the incision in the uterus. The nurse would clear any mucus from the pup's mouth and nose and stimulate the pup to take its first breath by rubbing it gently with a towel. We would all be eagerly listening for that first little squeak. It is very rewarding to have a box full of squeaking pups lying in a wriggling mass on a warm blanket placed over a hot water bottle. The only downside of a caesarean operation is the volume of birthing fluids which must be cleaned up from theatre afterwards, and the timing shown by many whelping bitches that are happy in first stage labour during working hours but get into difficulties and need veterinary help during the night.

Some procedures don't require surgery but are rewarding in a different way. Barley awns, the large, pointed seeds on long grass in the summer hedgerows or fields, often find their way into a dog's ear as the dog rushes through the meadow. The barley awns have a one-way trajectory and, once lodged down the ear canal, will not come out on their own; in fact, they will go deeper and deeper towards the eardrum and cause the poor dog tremendous pain. With some special forceps and an otoscope (a special magnifying glass), it is possible to remove a damaging seed with one deft action. This makes the pet feel better almost immediately and is immensely satisfying.

A cut paw or a cut ear on a dog may only be a small wound but can bleed profusely. The dog will run around shaking its head, leaving a liberal splattering of bright red blood over all the walls and cupboards, or it will run through the house over the pale cream carpets with bright red blood pouring out of its cut pad. I have even heard of the dog jumping on the bed and leaving a trail of bloody paw prints on the duvet. In these cases, cleaning and treating the wound and applying a bandage is important for the well-being of both the pet and the owner.

There are many joyous events that happen in the working day of a vet, but there are many sad times too. The loss of a pet can be incredibly hard for owners to bear, and emotions surrounding the loss of a beloved pet run high in vets too. I have felt very sad when deciding that a much-loved pet has reached the end of a long and treasured life. Knowing how strongly the loss will emotionally impact the owner is hard, but it can be a small comfort to know that the pet will no longer suffer. It is natural for owners to feel devastated when the life of their pet, a loved member of their family, comes to an end and giving comfort to a grieving owner is a natural extension of the trust one builds with a client.

Each year one of the vets in our practice attended Bakewell Show in the capacity of Official Show Veterinary Surgeon. We treated any of the wide variety of animals on the showground that needed help, whether they were competitors or just accompanying their owners on a day out. I would be given a walkie-talkie to carry with me, on which I would be called to a specific area of the show ground to see any animal in need.

"Could the vet make her way to the cattle lines" would be the sort of message I would receive. I would jump in my car and slowly inch my way along the walkways thronged with visitors. It was slower to drive than it would be to walk, but I needed to take my medicines and equipment with me, and the cattle lines were situated right across the far side of the showground from the vet's station. On this occasion, I was asked to examine the cow's udder in case she had mastitis. If she had this condition, she would have to be withdrawn from the competition and no longer be eligible to be shown in her class.

Another call was to the dog show where a dog had been stung by a bee. I had to attend to a horse that had injured its leg while jumping in a knockout jumping competition in the arena. I always carried a sterile suture kit and bandages, and these were put to good use on this horse. The wound was small and would heal but would mean an early homeward journey for that horse and rider.

An agriculture show is an opportunity for the farming community to showcase their best stock, and to be able to combine this with a day out with their farming friends is a bonus. Bakewell Show catered for horse owners too with show classes, heavy horses and show jumping competitions. The dog show was always busy and popular. For me, the day was a lovely opportunity to meet many clients and friends, but being on duty, it was not an opportunity to relax.

I did however manage to have a look around the produce stalls and the 'craft' stalls, and one year I remember being childishly pleased with a purchase of a lifelike rubber rat on wheels. It had a coil mechanism attached to the wheels so you could wind it up, and when released, it would move across the floor in a very realistic manner. I had a perfect plan for this rat. The next day back in the surgery, when my lovely colleague was sitting at reception, I stealthily put the rat on the floor near her chair and let it go.

"Watch out, Louise, what's that by your foot?" I asked innocently. The rat shot out from under the reception desk as if it was running up a drainpipe.

Louise shrieked, jumped up and jumped right up onto her chair,

"It's a rat; quick take it away!"

I knew I would have a heavy price to pay for that trick. And soon enough, I got my just deserts...

The following week when rampant rats were far from my mind, I had completed my morning consultations and was just about to start checking the repeat medication prescriptions. I had a list of phone calls waiting to be made, and I hadn't got a lot of time, but nature was calling, so before I did anything else, I had to visit the toilet. I walked into the room, lifted the toilet lid and nearly died.

There was the biggest, blackest spider I have ever seen, lurking in the toilet bowl. It must have been a good eight inches across. I squealed and ran out of the room as fast as I could.

As soon as I saw my staff convulsed with laughter, I realised the joke was on me this time. The spider was not real, but a horribly large and lifelike Hallowe'en trick purchased by the nurses who had tied it to the underside of the toilet seat to wait for me. Haha, it had certainly worked well.

Another amusing incident was the day my receptionist discovered a small circular tin that had been left behind on the counter in the waiting room when morning surgery had finished. When she opened it to investigate what was inside, she was more than a little surprised to discover a set of false teeth. This could present quite a problem to their owner; we didn't like to think of someone going hungry because they couldn't remember where they had left their teeth. So, we decided to look back through the list of clients who had visited us that day and see if, between us, we could guess who they might belong to. My receptionist could then ring each person in turn, starting with the person we judged most likely to be the rightful owner.

We scored full marks when the first person on our list turned out to be the grateful owner.

CHAPTER
TWENTY-NINE
MAGICAL MOMENTS

I n the depths of the dark night, you are suddenly awoken from a deep, all-encompassing sleep with such a start that your heart pounds as you fumble to turn on the light while the piercing sound of the all-invasive phone seems relentless, you ascend from unconsciousness to professional alertness and answer the call – a ewe having difficulty lambing, needs immediate help.

You climb out of your snug bed and into the many layers of clothes required for warmth on a dark Peak District dawn.

Into the car, it has taken only ten minutes from sublime slumber to waking, working mode.

When I arrive it is still dark, so I don my head torch and gather everything I need from the car boot. A bucket of clean, warm water is ready and waiting, this is a well-prepared farmer, and the lambing ewe is inside a semi-warm open-fronted building instead of several fields walk away.

She is in a pen in one corner of a clean three-sided barn, newly lambed ewes in the rest of the shed, nuzzling lambs and gently bleating. It is a timeless pastoral scene.

The farmer gently holds the ewe still while I feel inside her. I detect that the lamb will not be able to be delivered naturally and will need a caesarean.

We make a 'table' from four straw bales placed together, and I ask for two more buckets of warm water (I'll be lucky!) I return to the car and gather everything else I will need, including a pack of sterile surgical instruments. I shave the fleece using a modified hand razor purchased from Boots (I detected a strange look when I bought a razor and several packets of blades!) and inject local anaesthetic into the ewe's side. We lay her on her side on the bales, and the farmer holds her head. I clean the surgical site, put on a clean waterproof gown, covering my many layers of jumpers. I scrub my hands and arms and am ready to begin. The first cut goes right down her side, then I can feel the lamb, and with a few more cuts, I am able to pull him out into the world. I hand the lamb to the farmer, who ensures the newborn is breathing while I am checking back in the ewe where I can feel another lamb. I pull this one out too and feel in again; it's just like a lucky dip. And this time, we are lucky. There is a third lamb waiting to be born, and all are alive and soon struggling to find wobbly legs and bleating their first cries. I sew everything up and help the ewe up onto her feet as she wants to look after her triplets.

I raise my head, satisfied, and as I look across the valley, a brilliant orb appears over the horizon, bathing the hillside in golden sunlight; warmth spreads over us and caresses us all. It is magical. I am glad I was forced out of my bed at such an hour.

I clean up and repack my equipment into the car. Just time for breakfast, and then the "proper" day will begin.

CHAPTER THIRTY
OPERATIONS

An important part of training to be a vet is time spent during your university holidays working alongside a qualified vet in a veterinary surgery and learning about the myriad of topics that university courses don't have sufficient time to cover. 'Seeing practice' or Extra-Mural Studies (EMS) should be rewarding and enjoyable for both the vets and for the student. It is helpful for the vet to have another pair of hands to aid with tricky tasks. It is rewarding to teach practical skills to a willing student and beneficial to talk through the clinical cases with someone who is studying the most up to date techniques and theories. It can be companionable to share the car journeys with someone else who has a similar dedication to veterinary life.

Calls can take longer when you are teaching a student who may not yet have the experience to be quick at completing some tasks, but most vets welcome the opportunity for the mutually beneficial experience of taking an enthusiastic student around with them, and in my experience, most clients are very patient and understanding too.

One Christmas time, I had drawn the short straw of being on duty the evening our practice was due to enjoy the annual festive Christmas meal in a local pub. Late that afternoon, I received a call to visit a farm where one of their dairy cows looked 'hollow' and wasn't eating her 'cake'. Cake being the high-quality protein-rich food fed to dairy cows in the parlour. We had a very capable student Jean, 'seeing practice' with us at the time. She was a local girl and had helped at the practice for years starting from when she was still at school right through until when she joined us on an official placement from the university veterinary course. I was well acquainted with the farm that had requested the call as I made a regular two weekly visit to monitor the dairy herd fertility. The cow was waiting for us in the milking parlour. Jean and I examined her, took her temperature and listened carefully with a stethoscope to the different gurgles and rumbles emanating from her stomach, which can reveal a lot about a dairy cow's well-being. My ears pricked when I listened to the stomach on the left side of the cow

"Jean, what do you make of this?" I asked, "What can you hear?"

I watched as Jean put her stethoscope against the side of the cow just behind the rib cage and flicked the skin with her finger, then listened to the noise it created inside the cow.

"It's pinging. I can definitely hear pinging!" was her reply. "It must be a DA."

Jean was correct. The cow had a displaced abomasum or fourth stomach, a condition often referred to as a twisted stomach. With her fourth stomach no longer in the correct position, the cow had lost her appetite and would not be able to properly digest her food; she would soon lose weight and would produce less milk. The pinging noise that we could hear is quite characteristic of this condition.

Time was not on our side if we wanted to make the cow better and make it to our Christmas meal before everyone else had finished eating. This cow's condition wasn't an emergency, but I knew that if we could replace the stomach to its proper position right now, the cow would return to full health as soon as possible. If all went according to plan, she would be feeling as right as rain very soon, and her milk yield would get back up to its previous level.

"We can operate on her now if you've time, David," I said to the farmer, "Might as well do it while Jean and I are both here."

"Have you got a halter so we can tie her in the shed and get two buckets of clean hot water and a bale to use as a table, please?"

David soon had a halter on the cow's head and tied her to the railing in a barn with clean straw on the floor. I proceeded to shave an area on both sides of the cow, numb it using local anaesthetic, then clean and sterilise it. After laying out my sterile instruments and donning my clean waterproof gown, I cut into one side of the cow's abdomen and felt inside to locate the displaced stomach in its wrongful position too high up and on the wrong side of the cow. I literally pushed the stomach down to the floor of the abdomen. Jean, meanwhile, felt in through the incision on the other side of the cow and was able to locate and grasp the stomach and gently pull it up into its rightful position, where we stitched it in place to ensure it stayed where it belonged. Then we closed up the muscles and skin on both sides of the cow, cleaned her up, so she looked as good as new with a shaved patch and an identical row of large white stitches on either side. We had finished. This was a good job done in record time.

The cow had already started to eat some hay before we'd finished packing away our stuff, the farmer was delighted, and with a bit of speed, Jean and I might even have time for a quick shower to wash off the 'cow perfume' before racing out to our well-earned Christmas meal.

Having two veterinary surgeons on a farm working together does not happen very often, but it can be a pleasant experience to share a surgical operation or other sorts of jobs with your colleague. One of the very first displaced abomasum (or twisted stomach) operations I ever performed on a cow turned out to be a memorable experience in a rather unexpected way. One of the other vets from the practice and I were operating together on the cow. My colleague was standing on one side of the cow, and I was on the other. We were halfway through the operation to replace the displaced stomach to its correct position, and both stood with one arm up to our shoulders inside the cow's abdomen. One of us was pushing the stomach down, and one was feeling for the stomach and pulling it up to the correct place on the other side. I had just located Peter, my colleague's hand inside the cow, as he pushed the displaced stomach to me when our attention turned to the farmer who had moved on from recounting tales about his day and was now talking about his wife. He paused before he continued,

"It was afternoon when I got back from the market; trade had been brisk. I'd sold some stirks (young cattle), and they'd made a good price, so I was thinking life was good. I thought my wife and I could have a bite of tea and then go down the local for a pint to sort of celebrate a good sale. I got home and went into the house and thought I'll just go upstairs to change before milking and b------ me, what should I find in the bedroom but my wife in bed with my neighbour."

My colleague's eyes met mine across the cow's back, and we hurriedly looked away.

"Mmmm", I managed.

"Mmmm," said my colleague.

"That's the end of it; she's out of here."

"Mmmm" while we busied ourselves suturing the cow, not daring to glance up.

"I reckon it's been going on for a while."

The outcome was:

The cow recovered uneventfully, The marriage broke down, and the wife moved out of the farmhouse, but peace was regained several months later. The neighbour moved elsewhere. And that is all in the day of a vet.

CHAPTER THIRTY-ONE
PEDICURES

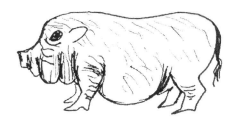

As I drove to the smallholding where Porky Pie lived, I experienced a wide spectrum of emotions. They ranged from curiosity to meet the Vietnamese Pot-bellied pig called Porky Pie, who needed her hooves trimming, to alarm at the thought of how that would be achieved. Pigs are lovely creatures; they are extremely intelligent; they are also very noisy. At the first whiff of a vet approaching with state-of-the-art hoof trimmers, they will back away, and as soon a soothing hand attempts restraint, they start to squeak, to squeal, in fact, to set up such an alarming noise that the neighbours rush out of their houses sure that someone is committing murder.

The trick is to deploy stealth. To convince Porky Pie that I really am here to offer her food. That no, we are not advancing on her with a small hurdle in order to pin her into the corner while, I, the vet, with deft precision, inject some sedative behind her ear. Then, if all goes well, we can wait in the peace and quiet. We can wait and twiddle our thumbs while Porky Pie becomes drowsy; she begins to sway slightly, her legs buckle, she grunts half to herself and then lies down in the straw bed. She looks asleep. Surely, she is sound asleep? If the unsuspecting vet is to rush in at this first sign of calm, there will be an almighty squeal, and Porky Pie will somehow stagger up onto those unsteady legs and lurch her large and solid frame around the pen. It is well known in the veterinary world that sedatives do not work very effectively when the animal is aroused or het up before they are injected. The animal needs to be quiet, to remain quiet and then to be injected. The drug will then work wonders. I know this through bitter experience. And so, we waited, Porky Pie, snoring in the straw, watched by her owner, the lovely, patient Amelia and by the impatient vet.

"Let's give her five minutes", I heard myself say, "and then she should be sleepy enough for me to trim all four of her feet."

Five minutes passed, although it felt a lot longer while we waited, and then we braved it. We walked towards the snoring black bulk lying in the pen. Quietly and with fingers crossed, we turned her onto her side. Perfect, she didn't even murmur. Quickly I gave her a pedicure. As the pet pig grows older and doesn't walk anywhere to wear her feet down, the horn of the hoof overgrows and causes discomfort. It can cause the poor pig to become lame. The hoof can crack and let infection track up into the foot, so it is important for health reasons that the hooves are kept the correct length. The job was soon completed. Porky Pie was beginning to stir and snuffle. Soon she was sitting up and looking around to see what had been happening while she was asleep. As she rose to her feet, I gathered up my equipment, ready to clean it before departing. A satisfied client and a satisfied vet, and a sleepy pig with tidy feet.

Foot trimming is an essential part of a mixed vet's workload. I didn't attend many pigs, but I saw a lot of lame cattle and a lot of lame horses.

One of my clients had a beef suckler herd, a herd where the cows rear their own calves until the calves are weaned, by which time the cow will be back in calf again. The cow has a rest period after her calf is weaned when she isn't producing milk, and the calf inside her grows and develops until she is ready to calve again. The farm I was going to visit on this occasion had two bulls that would both run with the cows to get them in calf when the time was right. Lame bulls are not keen on serving cows, and so it is vital that the bulls' feet are kept in good order so they are fit and ready to 'work' in the summertime.

Lifting up, examining and trimming the foot of a very large bull of uncertain temperament weighing more than a tonne can be tricky and somewhat dangerous. Great care is needed. Some farms have invested in a special 'crush' – a sort of cage designed to hold a cow and allow the foot to be raised and safely held in position. Unfortunately, many bulls are too large to fit into a crush, and I knew when I received the call to come and take a look at the lame bull that this farm didn't have a suitable crush. They did, however, have a small grass field that was level, and the ground was dry and would be perfect for sedating the bull so he would lie down and allow us to examine his feet. In theory, after injecting the massive bull with a calculated dose of sedative, we could turn him loose into the aforementioned paddock and watch him slowly get sleepier and sleepier so that after ten minutes he would lie down, and we would be able to examine and trim his foot.

So, first, the bull must be injected; this was safely carried out. The bull was walked slowly and successfully to the field. He loved it in this small paddock and immediately began to graze. We watched. I knew he would soon become wobbly and stagger forward, just as if he had spent the evening in the pub. He tottered around the field; he swayed across the middle of the field; he staggered far too close to the drystone wall enclosing the field.

"Oh no, if he falls on that, we're stuck, and the wall will be smashed", I worried.

"Phew, he's missed the wall." On he staggered, he was stumbling, swaying about to drop; any second now, he will drop to his knees and slowly sink onto his side, there he goes...

"He's not! He is! Oh heck!"

No one had noticed the telegraph post in the corner of the field carrying the phone line to this remote farm. Thump, the bull lurched forward and down into a lying position right up against the pole. The pole began to tilt; it went in slow motion, it tilted some more. And then, it stopped. It was leaning at a tremendous angle, but the wires were still several feet off the ground.

"Let's crack on with his foot. I think I'll be able to manage to pare it even though he's lying half up the pole," I spoke while running over to the beast so I could start on his foot as soon as possible.

Luckily, I soon found the infection that had tracked up into his foot from the sole and I was able to release the pus, which had been building up and causing a lot of pain. After paring the horn away to allow drainage and trimming the rest of the claw into a better shape, I was satisfied that he would soon feel a lot better and no longer be lame. We pulled the beast into a more upright position where he would be able to get back on his feet when the sedative wore off. Then we retired to a safe distance to ensure that he recovered with no further incident.

A few months later, I revisited the farm and saw the telegraph pole was still standing, but still at a rather jaunty angle to the ground.

CHAPTER THIRTY-TWO
BEING A VET IS NOT ALWAYS ENJOYABLE

W hen I am asked to examine any animal that has recently lost weight, I always make sure I check the condition of their teeth and mouth. We all know how painful toothache can be but add to that the problem faced by herbivores whose teeth continuously erupt or 'grow' and are worn down by the grinding action of the upper teeth on the lower teeth as the animal chews grass, hay or silage. In those unfortunate animals where for some reason, the teeth are not in perfect alignment, sharp projections form where part of the tooth in one jaw is insufficiently worn away by the opposing tooth. Over time these projections or points can develop into sizeable overgrowths, many of which are sharp and cause ulcers to form on the inside of the gums or tongue. I have spent a lot of time staring into the depths of a horse's mouth or stooping down to get a good view of the back teeth of a donkey. To enable a thorough examination of all the teeth, I would use a 'gag', which is like a bitless bridle with the addition of a ratchet mechanism enabling the mouth to be opened. Then armed with a brightly lit head torch, I could see into the very depths of the horse's wet, cavernous mouth. Holding the large fleshy tongue in one hand and moving it to one side would enable me to have a clear view and to feel if any of the teeth were sharp. Sometimes many teeth would be very sharp or have needle-like points on them. These called for action and would need rasping to make them smooth. If the overgrowths on the teeth were small, they would be able to be rasped with a hand rasp. In cases where there was a considerable overgrowth to remove, I would sedate the horse and use a power tool. This was particularly useful for large overgrown teeth at the very back of the mouth, which are more awkward to access. I saw a lot of donkeys with very overgrown teeth, which I don't think had ever previously been looked at. It was very satisfying to know that I was making the donkey a lot more comfortable and that they would be in much better health once they could eat properly.

From one end of the spectrum to the other, from large horses to donkeys and right down to rabbits, long, sharp teeth cause a lot of hardship. As you can imagine, looking into the very back of a rabbit's mouth can be quite challenging. You can get an idea that things may not be good in the dental department by examining the mouth in the consultation room, but to have a thorough examination, it is necessary to give the rabbit an anaesthetic and to open the mouth wide using a gag. This allows all the teeth to be seen and the lips, tongue and gums to be checked over. No animals can actually tell you what is wrong with them or where their pain is felt, but for animals like rabbits who are hunted by other animals in the wild and have learnt to hide how they feel, it can be especially hard to know when they have a problem. Combine this with the fact that many rabbits don't spend much time with their owners or get to know them very well (or is it the other way round?) dental problems may be missed until they are quite advanced, and the rabbit is very poorly.

I t is unusual to be bitten when examining a horse's mouth or a rabbit's! But I remember I was walking along the front of a row of stables one day carrying my dental equipment to attend to the horse in the end loose box. As I walked unsuspectingly past one box, the horse lunged forward and planted its teeth into the top of my arm. I shrieked with pain and astonishment. I hadn't ever been bitten by a horse before. I had a prize black and blue bruise on my arm for some while after that visit.

Usually, it was the other way round – I thought I might be kicked; in fact, I was almost expecting to be kicked by the cow or horse I was looking at, but they decided, after all, to be kind and spare me. Once I was taken completely by surprise during a visit to blood sample some hardy native breed of cattle with long shaggy hair and huge horns. They were all tied by the neck, standing side by side in their shed in two long rows, heads facing apart and backsides facing towards the centre of the shed where I had to walk and work. Blood samples in cattle are taken from the vein which runs on the underside of the tail, so I held the tail straight up in the air with one hand and took the blood sample via a sterile needle into a special tube with the other hand. I was standing facing the back end of one cow with another cow's backside behind me. I had no more than one foot of space to work in between the two cows, as I progressed along the line of cows, taking a sample of blood from each one in turn. Slowly I moved from cow to cow, holding my breath that I wouldn't have to jump sideways if one should kick out when I stuck the needle into her tail. There were about twenty cows in the shed, ten tied each side. I was halfway up the second side, breathing a sigh of relief when, bumph out of nowhere, the next cow along that I hadn't yet touched landed a heavy full-force kick on my thigh. I immediately felt nauseous and staggered sideways, knocking some of the filled blood tubes out of their box as I did so. My first thought wasn't about whether I had cracked my femur or not, but I heard myself say,

"Oh no, I hope the blood tubes haven't broken" I couldn't face sampling them again."

After a few minutes, I felt sufficiently recovered to find the spilt tubes and complete the sampling. Luckily all tubes had been labelled as soon as they were filled, so there was no confusion over which sample belonged to which cow. The tubes are plastic and hadn't broken when they fell, and more to the point hadn't been trampled by the cows. The astonishing sequel to that morning was that I never developed a bruise on my leg. I felt quite cheated that I had nothing to show for that painful kick.

Whilst writing this, I have been taken back to a time when I was blood sampling an entire herd of adult cows. They were well-behaved cows and were being run through the 'crush' cattle handling facility placed halfway down a large cubicle shed. The cows that were waiting to be sampled were standing on one side of a makeshift barrier, while the cows that I had already sampled were let out of the crush onto the other side of the barrier. I was working by the crush next to a wheelbarrow containing the blood-filled tubes labelled and placed in order in a special box. The paperwork recording which ear tag number corresponded to the label on each blood sample was attached to a clipboard in the wheelbarrow, in easy reach for me to write on. I vividly remember noticing a cow on my side of the barrier with something unusual in her mouth. What it was didn't dawn on me for a moment or two; I was too busy taking the blood from the next cow.

And then, all of a sudden, my stomach lurched. I raced towards the cow just in time to see the paper with all the ear tag numbers we had so far recorded disappear down her throat. She had pinched it out of the wheelbarrow and eaten it in its entirety. To say I was dismayed was an understatement. We had no way of telling which blood sample belonged to which cow. We had completed forty-five of the fifty samples. We couldn't resample them all again as the cows needed to get back out to grass. What was I to do?

In the end, all the samples tested negative, meaning none of the cattle had been in contact with the disease we were testing for. If there had been a different scenario and one or more had been positive, I would have had to test them all again. I had been lucky, and I think the moral is always to expect the unexpected when you work with livestock and take extra special care.

CHAPTER THIRTY-THREE

POLLY

Hens are wonderfully curious characters. They strut around an orchard quietly clucking to themselves then stopping, holding their head on one side as they listen to that worm in the grass and then down goes their head as they grab the tasty morsel from the soil. On a sunny day, when the light streams through the trees in shafts, the hens can be found indulging in dust baths. They find a dry bit of soil, scratch it up, settle down in it and fluff out their feathers. All this is thirsty work; they will drink clean water from wherever they can find it. An old bucket left out under the trees, which has filled with water, will be very attractive to a thirsty hen who will take a long drink to quench her thirst.

Hens can suffer from parasites, internal ones which cause diarrhoea and external ones which cause itchiness and feather loss and then progress to more serious skin disease. I have seen many cases of both, and diagnosing what is wrong at the time, treating the problem, then discussing how to prevent these diseases in the future can be very satisfying for the vet, as well as for the hen.

One afternoon a distressed owner arrived at the surgery with two small children and a large brown, very poorly chicken. The chicken had been caught by the neighbour's dog and was showing signs of clinical shock, and had a large skin wound on her back. This is actually a big understatement. Hen's skin is incredibly fragile, and when punctured savagely by the many sharp teeth in a dog's mouth, it will tear. In this case, it looked as though the hen was trying to take her whole skin off like taking off a coat. Her skin was split along the entire length of her back from neck to tail.

I was very afraid she would not recover, but I knew we would do whatever we could to save her. First, we made sure she was warm before we anaesthetised her using gaseous anaesthesia delivered by a face mask (or should I say beak mask) specially made for this chicken. Then I cleaned the wound and sutured it together using stainless steel sutures which you place using a surgical stapler. When I had finished, there were forty sutures holding the skin back in place.

Over the next few days, Polly, for that was her name, was looked after very well by the family. She was hand fed her favourite food, enticed to drink water, and she was allowed out on her own, strictly away from dogs. Ten days later, she came back to the surgery for her sutures to be removed. Her skin had healed completely, she was back to full health, and apart from a distinct lack of feathers along her back (imagine a 'reverse Mohican'), you wouldn't know anything untoward had happened to her. Polly was one brave little hen and very much loved by her owners.

One of the best memories for me was several weeks later receiving a printed photo of Polly looking proud and regal in her full plumage once more. On the back, the photo had been signed by the children with thanks.

It's not only hens who get injured and need putting back together again. One call-out was to a horse that had somehow impaled himself onto a stake of wood that had stuck into his chest and torn away a huge flap of skin and muscle. When I arrived, he had been brought in from the field where the accident had occurred and was now in the stable looking a very sorry sight. Blood was still dripping from the wound on his chest, the skin gaped open, and I could see a large hole where the post had damaged the muscles. I wanted the horse to remain standing while I examined, cleaned and sutured his wound, so I injected some sedative into his vein so he would remain calm during the procedure that would follow. Injecting pain relief, local anaesthetic, antibiotics, and anti-tetanus protection is important in these situations and then cleaning and examining the wound is crucial. A wound becomes infected and will not heal if a piece of stick, even a tiny piece, is left inside or bits of soil or gravel are not removed. I always carried kits of sterile drapes and surgical instruments as part of the equipment in my car, along with packs of sterile suture material, so when we were ready to start closing the wound, I asked for a straw bale to be put outside the stable door to act as a table for my surgical kit. The horse was well behaved, the sedative had worked well, and we were in a nice clean stable in broad daylight, not out in a muddy field at dusk with a gale howling around our ears. The two sisters who owned the horse were both helping me, and both were experienced in handling horses which can make my job a lot easier, especially when the task was a hard one like this.

I had cleaned the wound and started placing absorbable sutures in the muscle layer; these sutures would not have to be removed but would dissolve over a few weeks. I placed the first two sutures and all was going well. The anaesthesia was working well, so the patient hadn't flinched or tried to stamp his foot, making the task much harder. I was comforted by the fact that both Mary, who was holding the horse's head and Martha, who was helping cut the suture material after each stitch, knew what they were doing. And then I heard a thud.

"Oh dear, Martha's fainted," said Mary. "She never could stand the sight of blood."

Martha sat up; she was OK; she hadn't knocked her head on anything when she fell. She was dispatched indoors to recover with a cup of tea.

I continued stitching while Mary assisted, helping to

pass things to me and holding the horse's head. It was a long job; the cut was very large, one of the worst I can remember. But I hadn't bargained for what happened next.

"I don't feel well," said Mary. "I think I'm going to faint".

"Let the horse's head go right now and sit down outside the stable," I said. It might sound brusque, but I couldn't risk Mary fainting under the horse. She must move out of harm's way even if I had to continue alone. Very luckily, the horse didn't really need holding and stood as still as a rock while I finished the marathon stitch-up. Mary and Martha both felt fine by the time I had finished. I cleaned the newly closed wound, wiping away the blood from the horse's legs where it had run down during the operation. Where the blood had dripped down and coloured the straw, I spread clean straw (to stop further fainting episodes). I gathered together all my stuff, and finally, I stood up straight. Even though I am fairly short, it had been necessary to bend down for a lot of the time, and my back was pleased to straighten out again. I was pleased with how the job had gone, I hoped the large and deep wound would heal without complications, and I hoped the two sisters wouldn't be afflicted again when they looked at the scar over the coming days.

The wound healed very well, and after a few weeks of very limited but gradually increasing exercise, the horse was ready to compete in shows once again·

For me being a vet is as much about working with people as it is about working with animals. Animals are the introduction into the worlds and diverse livelihoods of their owners. Building trusting relationships with colleagues, farmers, horse and pet owners while working within so many diverse situations is a very special privilege, especially when it unfolds in the beautiful Peak District landscape. Every walk through the dales or over the moors, every shopping expedition to the local town or village comes alive for me with reminders of stories of life and work as a vet in this lovely area so full of community spirit. My work is part of who I am, in the same way that the people with whom I have shared the hard times, the laughter, the wild weather will always occupy a special place in my treasured memories.

About the Author

Lorna has always had a love of animals and an interest in people. As a child, the family enjoyed owning cats, dogs and later, ponies. A year working on a farm with prize-winning Hereford cattle firmly convinced Lorna that Veterinary Surgery was the career for her.

After gaining her degree from Liverpool University, Lorna's first job was in Oxfordshire, after which she moved to Bakewell, Derbyshire, to work in a more rural area. Lorna joined a small mixed practice then, with a colleague, purchased the business and built a new, modern surgery. She enjoyed many years working with the lovely people of this beautiful area, caring for their livestock and pets.

Lorna has now retired from clinical veterinary work but still lives in one of the stone villages typical of the Peak District.